D1532692

WITHDRAWN

VOICES FROM THE HEART

IN CELEBRATION OF AMERICA'S VOLUNTEERS

by **BRIAN O'CONNELL**

preface by **THOMAS MOORE**

project director
REBECCA BUFFUM TAYLOR

CHRONICLE BOOKS
San Francisco

A NOT-FOR-PROFIT JOINT PUBLICATION

JOSSEY-BASS PUBLISHERS
San Francisco

1828 L Street NW, Suite 1200
Washington, D.C. 20036
www.indepsec.org

Produced and edited by
Rebecca Buffum Taylor
Prose/Arts
Mill Valley, California
coyote99@ix.netcom.com
Research: Douglass Fischer
Project Coordinator: Jula Falvey

Designed by Carole Goodman and Anne Galperin

Library of Congress Cataloging-in-Publication Data available

Printed in Singapore
ISBN: 0-8118-2125-0 paperback 0-8118-2115-3 hardcover

10 9 8 7 6 5 4 3 2 1

Chronicle Books
85 Second Street
San Francisco, CA 94105

www.chroniclebooks.com

Jossey-Bass Publishers
350 Sansome Street
San Francisco, CA 94104

www.josseybass.com

ACKNOWLEDGMENTS

Largest possible appreciation is extended to Chronicle Books and Jossey-Bass Publishers for taking on this complicated joint project in the first place and then deciding to do it entirely as a pro bono effort.

Lynn Luckow, president of Jossey-Bass, initially took interest in a manuscript I had submitted on the subject and suggested it could be far more appealing and effective if the text were coupled with the photographs of volunteers in action. When I agreed, he talked with Jack Jensen and Caroline Herter, president and former publishing director, respectively, of Chronicle Books, the country's most prominent producer of illustrated books, and with their enthusiastic concurrence this different publication took hold.

Lynn and Caroline accepted leadership of the enterprise in their own organizations and as co-heads of it. They and their many associates who joined in this very large voluntary undertaking are grand examples of volunteers in action.

To assist in coordinating and meshing the different operations and styles of the two publishers, as well as my role as author, we were fortunate in attracting as project director and editor Rebecca Buffum Taylor, who is masterful at achieving harmony and wholeness out of many different parts and personalities. Lynn and Caroline readily join me in thanks and praise to her.

We are grateful to Thomas Moore for providing a preface that is a very special message on its own and an inspiring introduction to the book and to the volunteers portrayed in it.

We want also to provide specific recognition to the following individuals who combined the best of professionalism and voluntarism:

At Jossey-Bass, thanks to Alan Rinzler, Erik Thrasher, and Carol Brown.

At Chronicle Books, thanks to Carole Goodman, Anne Galperin, and Vanessa Brown.

Appreciation for special assistance is also extended to INDEPENDENT SECTOR, especially Sara Melendez and John Thomas, the Points of Light Foundation, especially Bob Goodwin and Ken Allen, and the Lincoln Filene Center at Tufts University, especially Sandi Gasbarro, and the funders who support my work there, the Kellogg, Ford, and Packard foundations, and an anonymous donor.

Love and thanks as usual to Ann B. O'Connell, who as always provided the wonderful combination of personal encouragement and professional assistance.

The following pages provide a listing of special funders for the project whose support helped cover unavoidable expenses even in a pro bono effort and kept the cost of the book as low as possible to be sure it is within reach of all individuals and organizations for whom it is intended. Special gratitude goes to Skip Rhodes of Chevron Corporation for providing the lead gift and encouraging other funders to join this important cause.

Thanks also to the great many people and organizations who provided services, supplies, and other assistance pro bono or at greatly reduced rates.

Lastly and particularly, appreciation and admiration to the people and associations who consented and cooperated in our portraying them in action. This extra volunteer effort on their part amplifies their voices from the heart.

Brian O'Connell

WITH SPECIAL THANKS to the organizations and foundations whose generous contributions and commitment made this book possible:

The James Irvine Foundation
The Robert Wood Johnson Foundation
Ewing Marion Kauffman Foundation
W. K. Kellogg Foundation
The John D. and Catherine T. MacArthur Foundation
The Charles Stewart Mott Foundation

American Heart Association
AT&T Foundation
Chevron Corporation
William Randolph Hearst Foundation
The David and Lucile Packard Foundation
MetLife Foundation
Mobil Foundation, Inc.
Levi Strauss & Co.
Tiffany & Co.

ARCO Foundation
California Community Foundation
The Chase Manhattan Foundation
The Cleveland Foundation
Family Service America, Inc.
John and Marcia Goldman Philanthropic Fund
Evelyn and Walter Haas, Jr. Fund
J.C. Penney Company, Inc. and The National 4-H Council
Albert Kunstadter Family Foundation
Local Initiatives Support Corporation
Mandel Family Philanthropic Fund
McKesson Foundation, Inc.
National AIDS Fund
National Council of La Raza
Oakleaf Foundation
The Points of Light Foundation
Presbyterian Health Foundation
Rosenberg Foundation
Save the Children
Xerox Foundation

In addition, our heartfelt thanks to the project's in-kind sponsors:

Techni-Graphics, Inc.
The Tides Center
TWP America, Inc.

CONTENTS

PREFACE

THOMAS MOORE

People say they are looking for happiness, but happiness is usually a passing sensation. As a way of life, it always seems out of reach. What we may be looking for is something deeper, some fulfillment of our potential, experiences, perhaps, that we can look back on and say to ourselves, "Life has been worth living."

In the temper of the times we turn inward when we look for this kind of meaning. We develop skills and talents, try yoga and meditation, and buy any new gadget that promises deliverance from the ennui of modern living. With many exceptions to the rule, we have forgotten that turning outward and making a positive contribution to our family, our community, and the world at large may provide that meaning and purpose without which we feel aimless and empty.

Over the years I have sat in therapy with many men and women whose chief complaint was loneliness. They felt it bitterly and did crazy things to chase it away or fill the emptiness. In those painful moments of dialogue, I would avoid psychological analysis and instead ask if there were someone, a child or a sick person in the family or neighborhood perhaps, who needed attention. Loneliness is not always resolved by finding a partner or a group of friends—you can be very lonely in a crowd of people—but by becoming absorbed in service to nature and community.

We are a profoundly egocentric culture. Popular psychology recommends a strong sense of self, well-maintained ego boundaries, and wholesome self-esteem—all ego concerns that turn our attention inward and increase anxiety. The religious and spiritual traditions offer a completely different point of view. They say that we find our soul only when we lose our highly prized sense of self. As Jesus said, "Finding his soul he loses it; losing it because of me he finds it."

The pleasure we are looking for that makes sense of life and provides the feeling of being grounded comes from a deep place—not from the surface ego but from the deep soul. We could spend our lives at the complicated project of making a healthy ego, but real satisfaction comes as a grace from the depths. And often it comes in paradoxical ways. The *Tao Te*

Ching says: "The sage never tries to store things up. The more he does for others, the more he has. The more he gives to others, the greater his abundance."

Spiritual sayings like these could be taken sentimentally and not mean much for practical living. On the other hand, they could offer a radically different philosophy of life, wherein we give up the entire effort of modern psychology to manufacture a conflict-free existence and instead discover an intense and deep sense of identity and purpose in service to others. Service is not just something we do out of the goodness of our hearts or from principle; it is a deep, archetypal experience of the soul, for which we have both a need and an instinct. Satisfying this need fulfills us at the very same time that it contributes to the world.

There is another paradox to be found in service, one that volunteers discover quickly. The real beauty of nature and of persons is often revealed within the ugliness of pain and suffering. One motivating reward for the volunteer is to discover the beauty and grace hiding beneath the veneer of suffering and deprivation.

The ancient Greeks told a mysterious story about this paradox. The great goddess of civilization, Athena, played the flute, but she hated the way it made her face contort, so she threw it away. Marsyas, a silenus—an ugly character with the ears and feet of a horse—picked it up and became a virtuoso with his own less cultivated style of music. One day he entered a contest with the magnificent Apollo, epitome of fine culture and the divine inventor of music. Naturally Marsyas lost, and Apollo ordered him to be skinned alive.

The nymphs of nature, the rustic spirits, cried over their comrade's pain until their tears made a river, but later poets saw the story more symbolically. Marsyas became an image for the interior life. Plato described his hero Socrates as a Marsyas figure: like a silenus figurine in shops, said Plato, on the outside he is ugly but on the inside he is full of gods.

The many moving stories of volunteers in this book tell how often their jobs involve interaction between the clean and polished world of Apollonic culture and the less pretty world of need and disadvantage. City kids go hiking in the forest and find a deep education there. A highly competent woman with a mastectomy is kept out of a job in Apollo's world of schools and discovers new life in less exalted settings. A rescue worker finds beauty in tragic circumstances of loss and death.

A volunteer can't worry about how she looks when she enters the terrain of human suffering. There is no place for Athena's pride, and the doctrine of no-self applies all the way. The volunteer chooses to cross the border between the surface delights of the protected life and the inner beauty of raw human existence.

With courage and heart the volunteer may surrender free time, personal security, and attention to self in service that often appears unremarkable. But the reward is immeasurable because it fills the heart and soul rather than the wallet or the ego. The volunteer is granted a vision of deep human beauty and grace that is covered over to the person unwilling to get that close to life without a personal agenda. And this vision is transforming. It offers the elusive joy and happiness that others often expect to find in inadequate, less humble substitutes.

It's interesting to notice how the many attractions and preoccupations in modern life contrast precisely with the concerns of the volunteer. Many people look for pleasure in the endless supply of technological gadgetry that industry continues to provide. While the volunteer is on the streets or in the woods, the rest of us sit in front of televisions and computer screens. "Tele-vision" means "seeing at a distance." The volunteer is in the midst of life and therefore finds personal vitality in service. The television addict looks at life through a glass partition, at a safe distance, and develops a strange numbed interpretation of life.

Apollo was called the "far-shooter." He, too, kept his distance. Marsyas was sometimes linked with the wilder Dionysus. The Dionysian life is involved and intimate. I am led to think that volunteering is one of the best therapies in our society. Through active and giving involvement in our own communities and around the world we break through the dominant neurosis of our age—the emptiness we feel from the protective distance with which we view life today.

Everyone could and should be a volunteer. To be paid for service is certainly legitimate, but it doesn't have the personal effect that the volunteer enjoys. Volunteering is a stepping out of the supposed prudent ways of smart society and entering life through another door. It isn't a way of helping as much as it is a way of being.

In stores I often find my books in a section labeled self-help. I have serious problems with both words. "Self," no matter how carefully defined, is inseparably linked to ego. I prefer the ancient word "soul" because it addresses both the important sense of "I," identity, and other. I also have trouble with the idea of helping. I don't see how to remove from that word a feeling of superiority. Sometimes people offer to help me in various ways, and if I haven't asked for help, I usually get a sinking feeling. I feel nudged deeper into my inferiority. So as a therapist and a writer, I try to keep my intentions clean. I don't start out with the idea of helping. If help happens, I guess that is all right.

I see a volunteer more as an adventurer than as someone pursuing a helping avocation. The volunteer has a good balance between service and self-realization. He or she enters more fully into life, and I assume that the desire for vitality inspires the volunteer. If all we do is do our paid work and see the side of experience limited by our social class and ethnic background, we only half live. The volunteer sees the promise for a fuller life in deeper engagement. The people he "helps," as any volunteer might confess, are usually his teachers.

The volunteer takes seriously and puts into simple, concrete practice the wisdom of the ages. The Self is neither within nor without, say the Upanishads. Just as salt dissolved in water spreads its taste everywhere, so the soul permeates everything. Accordingly, the volunteer finds her soul in the little world she pours herself into. The volunteer also disregards the modern idea that we are all independent atoms living in our isolated neighborhoods and homes. The volunteer doesn't argue the point, but lives out the philosophy that sees us all profoundly connected and mutually dependent. "Every atom belonging to me as good belongs to you," says Walt Whitman. Or, in the unsurpassed words of John Donne, who gradually found his way from a life of abandon to one of service as a father of seven and a pastor of countless souls:

Every man is a piece of the continent.
A part of the main.
Any man's death diminishes me,
Because I am involved in mankind.

INTRODUCTION

IN CELEBRATION OF AMERICA'S VOLUNTEERS

BRIAN O'CONNELL

This book honors every American who is a volunteer and provides inspiration and guidance for those not yet involved. We want to impress on everyone how important volunteers are to the people, causes, and communities served, and to the kind of caring nation we can be.

One hundred million citizens already volunteer. That's a staggering one out of every two of us over the age of thirteen. It is essential to our personal morale and to our pride as a nation that all of us recognize and rejoice in the fact that we the people still care and still make an enormous difference on every conceivable aspect of the human condition.

A society is what it reveres, and this book is an acknowledgment and celebration that volunteering is one of the most distinguishing and distinguished features of American society.

Our story is told primarily through the portraits of twenty-five volunteers, including their own words about what they do, why they do it, and what the experience has meant to them. Their reasons and impressions cover the full range of human motivations and rewards, but what comes through repeatedly is that they like being able to make a difference, feel good about themselves for doing it, gain new skills and confidence, meet and become friends with fascinating people who are also making the effort, and they feel the experience adds new dimensions to their lives in many other rewarding ways.

Let's listen to a few of their voices:

Scott Rosenberg, for example, is an artist who teaches at-risk teenagers to produce films and videos. He describes the experience like this: *On a visceral level, volunteering is a natural high. You get lifted in the right way when you work with people on something you believe in. It's arduous work, but you come away feeling exhilarated.*

Valdimir Joseph, a college counselor, founded Inner Strength, which provides mentoring for young African-American men. He says: *Everyone has something to offer. Working with other volunteers has helped give me strength. They are struggling, too. I feel empowered watching volunteers develop relationships with these kids, watching them both grow. . . . Everyone I've met who volunteers, even if they only do two hours a week, makes a difference in someone's life.*

Amber Coffman, a teenager, provides food to the homeless and summarizes her reaction: *It's about changing people's lives because of a few volunteers who get together on weekends and just give from the heart. That's what gets me up early when I don't feel like making lunches. I do it because of the wonderful feelings involved with giving. Once you truly give of yourself, you're hooked for life.*

John Gatus, a retired steamfitter, supervises an anti-gang street patrol and reflects: *Volunteer work brings real change, change you can be a part of, change you can see with your own eyes. You don't need politicians or the police to tell you things are better. You can see it and feel it for yourself, and know you were a part of it. . . . There's real pride involved. We're part of the community.*

Katherine Pener has counseled post-surgery breast cancer patients for 22 years and proclaims: *I guarantee anyone who volunteers will feel better emotionally, physically, and psychologically. I don't care who you are or what you do. The people I know who volunteer have smiles on their faces. The hours they give are worth more to them than any money they could ever receive.*

Karen Von den Deale emphasizes: *I wish I would have started much sooner. I feel like I've wasted a lifetime.*

Karen's regret about not getting involved sooner shows up

in many of the portraits. It also comes through in studies of those who are not yet participating. Indeed it's fascinating and encouraging that people not involved also believe in volunteering. They hold the same good values as volunteers, they believe in paying back, and they even envy those who are involved. The major reasons they're not already participating are that they have not been asked in a personal way or they don't know how to get started on their own. For them and for those who want to be more involved there is a special guide toward the end of the book.

We believe that this celebration of volunteering, including the portraits and the wonderfully encouraging facts about volunteers and volunteering, will reinforce the commitment of those already involved and spread the participation to an even larger proportion of citizens.

There's something wonderfully rewarding in being part of an effort that makes a difference. When any of us take inventory of the meaning of our lives, the occasions of making a difference for other people and for important causes turn out to be among our lasting joys. And there's something rewarding in being among other people when they're at their best, too. Happiness is, in the end, a simple thing. Despite how complicated we try to make it or the entrapments we substitute for it, happiness is caring and being able to do something about it.

In the community sense, caring and service are giving and volunteering. As far back as the twelfth century, the highest order and benefit of charity were described by Maimonides in the Mishna Torah: "The highest degree, than which there is nothing higher, is to take hold of a Jew who has been crushed and to give him a gift or a loan or to enter into partnership with him or to find work for him, and then to put him on his feet so he will not be dependent on his fellow man."

The problems of contemporary society are more complex, the solutions more involved, and the satisfactions more obscure, but the basic ingredients are still the caring and the resolve to make things better. From the simplicity of these have come today's exciting efforts on behalf of humanitarian causes ranging from equality to environment and from health to peace.

In the course of these efforts, there is at work a silent cycle of cause and effect that I call the "genius of fulfillment," that is, the harder people work for others and for the fulfillment of important social goals, the more fulfilled they are themselves. Confucius expressed it by saying, "Goodness is God," meaning that the more good we do, the happier we are, and the totality of it all is a supreme state of being. Thus, he said, God is not only a Supreme Being apart from us, but a supreme state of being within us.

A simpler way of looking at the meaning of service is a quotation from an epitaph:

What I spent is gone
What I kept is lost
But what I gave to charity
Will be mine forever.

How we express the meaning of volunteering doesn't really matter. It can be charity or enlightened self-interest or humanity to others. These are all ways of describing why people volunteer, why volunteering provides some of their happiest moments, and why the good that we do lives after us.

So enter the celebration—look, read, and enjoy. Listen to these voices from the heart.

As Walt Whitman described it, listen to America singing.

VALDIMIR JOSEPH

COLLEGE COUNSELOR, AGE 24 **ATLANTA, GEORGIA**

Founder of Inner Strength, which provides mentoring for young African-American men

PHOTOGRAPHS BY PAUL FUSCO

My parents divorced when I was seven, so I stayed with my mom, a hard-working lady. My pops, he was a jerk. A lot happened between them when I was young. My mom got some sense, got a divorce, and moved out with the kids. She struggled a long time trying to raise me and my sister. By the time I was eleven, she was having crazy stress, and I started hanging out in the streets.

One day I came home and all the furniture was gone. No one ripped the place off; she had moved out without me.

I stayed with my pops until he kicked me out. I was thirteen and homeless, but I knew my way around. A week after my fourteenth birthday, I got into a turf mishap. I was hit on the head with a crowbar on a rooftop. I used to scout out rooftops to sleep on. I could just chill up there. But I was attacked one day up there, knocked out, and put into a hospital. When I got out, I was put into a shelter for a while and that got me back into school.

In the mornings, I went to high school and kept all my clothes in my locker. I'd wash up and shower there. I loved school. I could be myself and kick some academic ass; it was cool. I could exchange ideas and be safe. I was on the football, wrestling, and track teams.

A counselor took a bunch of kids upstate, on the Appalachian trail. Seeing the clouds, the trees—no boom boxes or urine smell—did something for my head. It was downtime to get into myself. It made me a firm believer in hiking.

In eleventh grade, I was in a gang and these guys from a rival gang were going to get rid of me. Move me off the planet. I didn't bother people,

"Kids need to get away from crack dealers, pimps, the brick life—places where they're forced to be adults," says Val. "Once they get out of that, they laugh and giggle and have fun. In nature, kids can be kids."

but I had my gun and got caught by the police. It was the same day I got my class ring. If I didn't get locked up right then, I probably would have had to kill someone an hour later. Those were mad times then, crooked cops, friends dying. It was nothing to see people die on the street.

The group home I stayed in was run by a Catholic priest. He knew I wanted to grow up and be a strong black man and suggested a lot of colleges for me. I had a few scholarships to other schools, but I chose Morehouse College. It was good to get out of the South Bronx. In my environment, the only successful black men were running guns and crack. At Morehouse, the students' dads were judges and professors.

I had three jobs to support myself. I had class in the mornings, then I ran a pool, taught swimming, and was a lifeguard.

"We have to be the family for the young people we help," says Val. "We've got to show love, because if it's not us, it'll be people on the street." Here Brya Wooden, Jacobi Hill, Yuseff Langford, and Val reach the top of Big Scaly Mountain in Georgia.

We've witnessed that when you take a kid out of his environment and bring him to a different place and challenge him to look at himself in a different way, change becomes tangible. It's possible. You sit in the ghetto and tell him, "You know you've got to do something," and he'll say, "Yeah, whatever." On a hike, I tell the kids that we are going to accomplish something today. It will be a long, hard road, but we are going to do it together. We are going to eat together, hurt together, but we are going to do it.

Coming from a dirty environment myself, I knew it would really impact the kids. Hiking is also good for group dynamics, sharing, staying together.

On one of our first overnight trips, a kid broke down crying. He said, "My mom's cracked out, and I don't know how to deal." He was crying out for help. As his "other" family, we can offer tangible support, not messed-up advice he'd get out on the street.

I didn't get money for the Inner Strength program until 1996. I was still doing construction then. "The group" was just me for a while. I would go and find people to help out. Food for the trips back then came from my pocket—I just brought bread, peanut butter, and water. The kids called them "sawdust sandwiches." Then friends and different church groups donated supplies. Morehouse also helped; they donated a van and driver to pick up kids. People were responsive, encouraging. Now it's a real organization. I had to learn about grant writing. We have to think as a business to survive. Funders want to see outcomes.

We thrive on creating a safe space where kids feel it's okay to be vulnerable and ask questions. It's tough because kids you help can fall off and go to jail. But we keep in touch and let them know that when they come out, we'll be here to help them. A lot of families will cut those kids off forever after jail. Kids need to know they have second chances.

Semester to semester, we now have between twenty and thirty college students volunteering from Morehouse, Spelman, Morris-Brown, and Clark-Atlanta. The best thing they can share is how they stayed out of trouble. Every one of these kids has someone in his neighborhood who is a drug dealer and will help them get into that life if they want to. But we provide an option. Kids bring in other kids, and trust enough in what we're doing to share it with their friends, even if their friends think it's corny.

Even after I started Inner Strength, I wanted to give up on myself sometimes. It was just too much—my life, three jobs—I wanted to quit. It was hard enough trying to maintain myself. Going through everything I did helped me realize my strength.

There's a quote from Booker T. Washington that I read to the kids sometimes: "Man is not judged from the heights that he has attained, but from the depths from which he has come." A lot of people feel they don't have time to volunteer, that they have to get money now. But think about five years from now. Think about how much more of an achievement you will have made if you can give while working toward your personal goals.

Everyone has something to offer. Working with other volunteers has helped give me strength. I feel empowered watching volunteers develop relationships with these kids, watching them both grow.

I learn so much about myself working with youth. Everyone I've met who volunteers, even if they only do two hours a week, makes a difference in someone's life. They're people of good character.

"I ate at soup kitchens when I was homeless," says Val. "I knew when I got the chance, I would do what I could for other young black men." Yuseff Langford, one of the young men on the hike, says of the program, "The nature part of Inner Strength takes you to a whole 'nother dimension. It gets you in another mind frame. We start out with our street selves but in the mountains, it's peaceful."

THERESA TOWNLEY

PHYSICIAN, AGE 33 **MINNEAPOLIS, MINNESOTA**

Provides medical care in the former Yugoslavia

PHOTOGRAPHS BY ALEX MAJOLI

Helping the people of another country was always a goal of mine. My family is pretty internationally aware and let us know we were lucky to have all of life's basic necessities.

When I said I was going to volunteer for Doctors Without Borders, they weren't surprised. But when they heard I would go to the former Yugoslavia, they were worried that I would put my life at stake in an unstable environment.

I didn't know much about Serbia. The Balkans situation was very muddled to me before coming here. I told Doctors Without Borders I wanted to go somewhere in South America because I speak Spanish. When they told me of the opening in Serbia, my first reaction was that I was kind of scared to go because of the war in Bosnia. That war was so unclear as to what was going on and who was on what side.

I've been in the southern region of Serbia since last July.

In Kosovo, there's tension between the two main ethnic groups—the Serbs and Albanians. The Serbs are mostly Orthodox; the Albanians, most of the population, practice Islam or Roman Catholicism. The international press makes it a religious battle—Islam versus the Orthodox church, but I think it's more ethnic than religious.

Kosovo is very unstable politically. It's been that way for a long time. The tension has intensified since I've been here, and it has the potential to continue to explode.

When I first got here it didn't affect my volunteer work, but now there have been student demonstrations. Albanians want classes to be taught in Albanian, not Serbian. University and high school

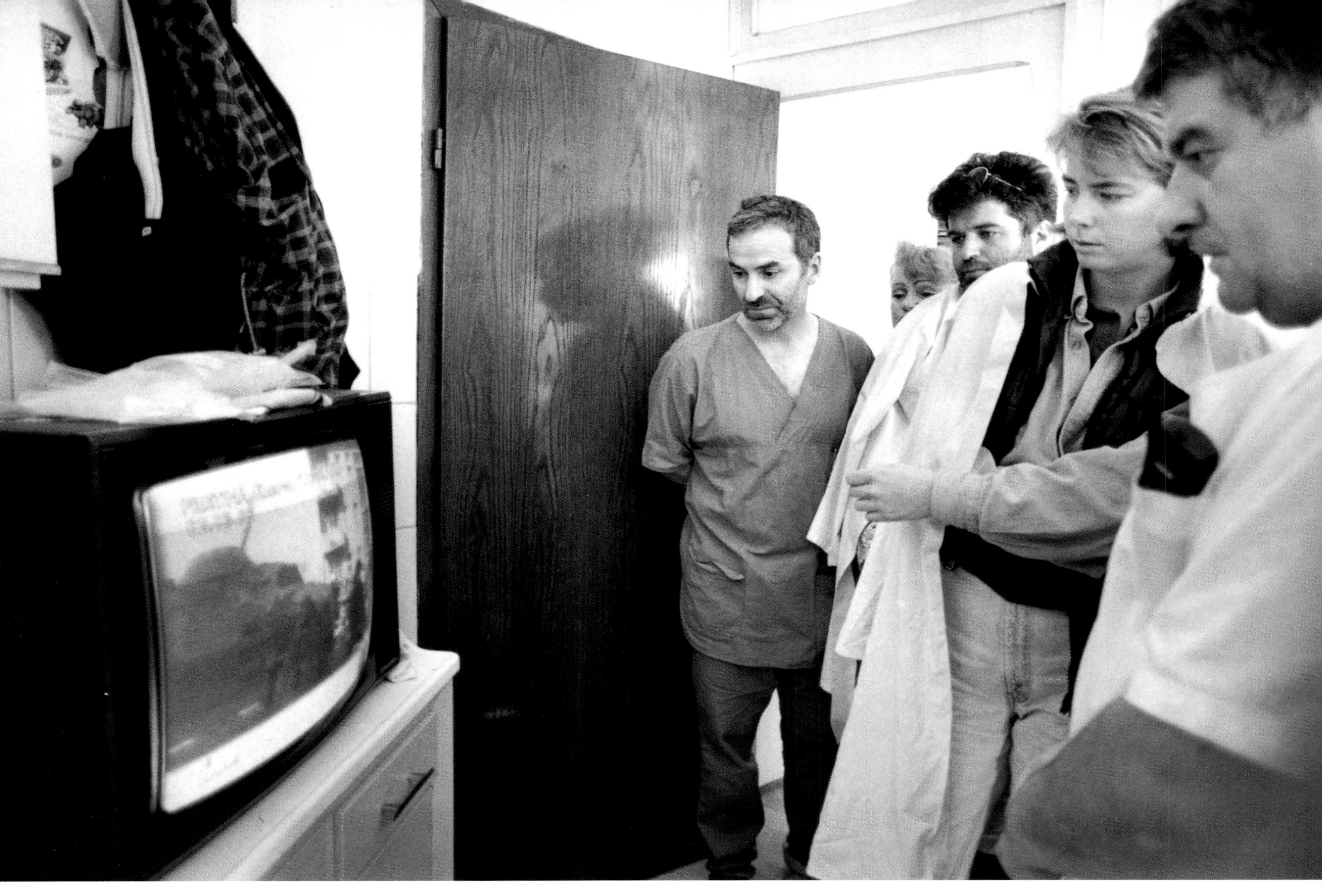

As violence erupts on March 2, 1998, Theresa (center) and other volunteer physicians watch local news reports of the widespread fighting between Albanian demonstrators and Serbian riot police in Pristina, where the volunteer doctors are living. Theresa and her colleagues risked arrest by Serbian police for traveling to visit clinics during the crisis.

students basically go to classes in private housing. The demonstration on October 1, 1997, was broken up with violence from the Serbian police—tear gas and sticks, tanks and militia men.

Around two hundred people were injured that day, but nobody died. We gave out medical emergency kits to the local doctors, to support them.

This past month, tension has really escalated. We've had to be more careful with our medical supply distributions. There are more checkpoints where people are stopped and questioned. We're

Theresa evaluates an infant in the pediatric hospital and visits a patient in the Mother Teresa Mission. Theresa was in Kosovo for nine months with Doctors Without Borders (Médecins Sans Frontières), a nonprofit international medical relief organization.

continually increasing our level of security, and it interferes with our medical work.

Generally, we're well accepted by officials and "unofficial" officials. We want to bring the two communities together. We want to build bridges. The vaccination program we have is improving the state's old system. In the early 1990s, people had tremendous fear that the state's polio vaccine contained toxins—so people didn't go through with it. In 1996, there was an outbreak of polio in over a hundred children, including some in Albania. They have permanent paralysis to various degrees; some aren't able to walk. Most were fairly young when the epidemic hit. Even now, most are under five.

I put in twelve hours a day—typical doctor hours. A typical day for me is going to clinics to distribute drugs and to get a better assessment of the needs in the area. Aside from being politically unstable, this area, unfortunately, is also economically depressed. Essential drugs and basic primary care are not available, so we're trying to improve the quality of care. There is no system of ongoing medical education, so we fill that need. The doctors here graduate without the good, practical training they would have had in the past. Medical school is carried on in private houses.

I have five sisters and four brothers. Three of us are doctors, three are nurses, my dad's a doctor, my mom's a nurse. Internationally and locally, we volunteer. I have a sister with Vita Volunteers—she's a public health nurse in Colorado—and a sister with the Jesuit Volunteer Corps. Most of my family has volunteered with a project in the Dominican Republic, and I also spent two months in Guatemala.

Volunteering in foreign countries is tremendously rewarding and, at times, emotionally straining. You forge relationships. You get attached. You become imbued with the people's struggle, and it's hard to leave that. You learn to look at the world through their eyes. In the Dominican Republic and Guatemala, my lifestyle was quite a bit different than the way it was growing up. It was difficult to go back to the materialism I knew. But because of those experiences, it's much easier to realize what is important in life. When I leave Kosovo, it will be nice to be away from such an ethnically intense area, but it will be hard getting used to the States again.

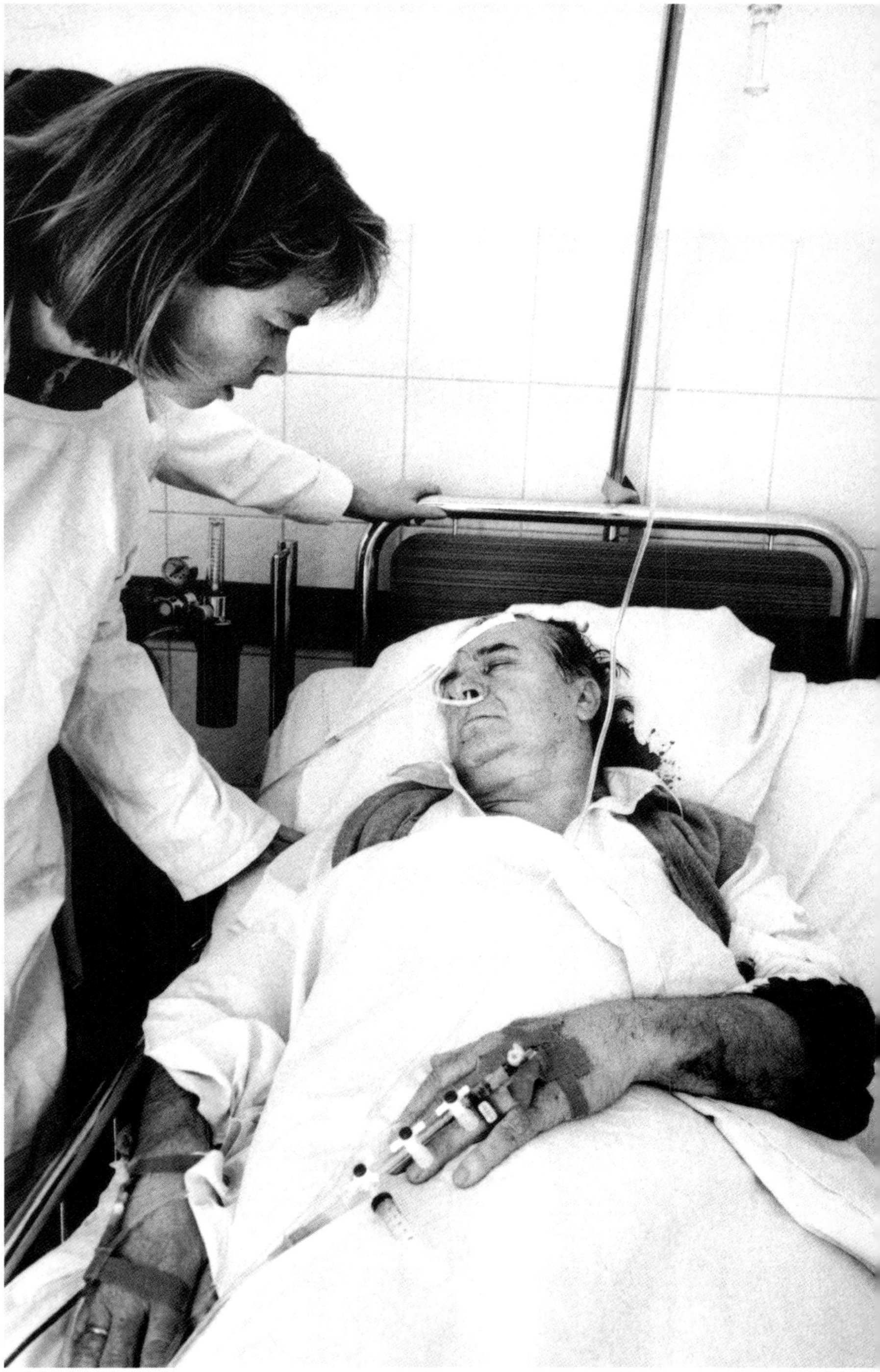

I see volunteerism as an extension of my medical work. I'm very grateful for organizations like Doctors Without Borders, because they give aid to victims of conflict and also let the world know of their plight. They bring attention, on an international level, and the more attention, the more diplomacy that can be brought, and perhaps we can avoid a war. Hopefully, we are doing some preventive work. Who knows?

This place may explode at any minute. But it is also a place of tremendous hospitality.

The other night I was on a late drive to Belgrade, traveling with an Albanian driver, and the car broke down. Serbs stopped to help. They even invited us back to their apartment to see their baby. Politically, situations may be very tense, but on a personal level, people are still giving, still willing to stop and help and show cooperation.

I learn so much from the people I work with. Instead of giving up, they continue to work, continue to do what they do in spite of the adversity. I witness this tremendous strength among people when it would be much easier to just give up. It's a tremendous opportunity to witness the resilience and ingenuity of the people around me.

During an especially violent week in March of 1998, Theresa tries repeatedly to contact her family in Omaha, Nebraska, but is unable to get through. Days of continual ethnic violence made the always difficult satellite-phone communication from Pristina impossible.

CARMINE ANTONELLE

SANITATION WORKER, AGE 49 **QUEENS, NEW YORK**

Raises funds and organizes events for disabled kids

PHOTOGRAPHS BY PAUL FUSCO

We've been riding for quite a while. We're not what you would call "enthusiasts," you know, lawyers or business executives who are into Harleys. We were riding twenty-five years ago, when guys wore the chains, the leather, and the beat-up boots.

Our group, Independent Bikers of Queens, is known mostly for our annual Toy Run, but we do a lot of other things. We're coaches and "big brothers" for participants in the Queens Special Olympics, and we take patients to see the Harlem Globetrotters, Disney On Ice, and the Barnum & Bailey Circus. We're about thirty guys and ladies. We meet every week at My Place Your Place Bar. Months before the Toy Run, the group grows to about seventy-five people. We don't just raise money for children, either, because handicapped children become handicapped adults.

There's a place, the Creedmore Psychiatric Center, where nobody ever visits because it has some criminally insane patients along with the disabled. We decided to check it out. The administration said we could throw the residents a Halloween party, and once we got around in the place, we recognized kids we gave toys to years ago who were now grown adults. One guy, Robbie, was twenty-two. He had been there for two or three years, always asking the nurses, "When will the motorcycle guys come by to give us toys?" The nurses had no idea what he was talking about until we showed up.

Most people jump on the volunteer bandwagon around Thanksgiving and Christmas. We do this year-round. We've been doing it for seventeen years, and it gets bigger and better every year. When we started, we raised about $200 in cash and toys. Last year we raised $27,000, and in

"We're not some political group," says Carmine (left), with Dean McNamee, co-chair of Independent Bikers of Queens, NY (far right), and other friends. "We're just trying to do what's right and bring some happiness into people's lives."

1995, a total of $80,000 was donated to the club. Everyone in our group is a total volunteer. We give our time and our hard work to the disabled residents of the Bernard Fineson Developmental Center. We do everything to raise money. We hold raffles and fund-raisers, solicit grants from foundations, sell biker souvenirs like T-shirts, bumper stickers, patches, lighters, key chains, everything. And every dollar raised goes to the kids.

"Nothing can bring you down when you do this kind of work," says Carmine, ready to lead 6,000 bikers in the Toys for Tots Run parade past 15,000 spectators. "As long as people you help believe in you, nothing can stop you."

TOYS FOR TOTS

What do we do with the money? We do whatever improves the quality of life for the disabled kids. We've given them new basketball and shuffleboard courts, two swimming pools, exercise equipment, hospital beds, wheelchairs, recreation stuff, you name it. One year, we asked the administrators what they could use. They said a sun shelter. Many folks, because of their disability or the medication they're on, can't go out and enjoy a sunny day. This was the first year we raised some real money, almost $10,000, so we said, "Okay, let's go for it," and we built the shelter. And I mean we built it. Like I said, we can do anything. I ordered fifty-three yards of concrete, and we laid it out. It's a place where they can go and get out from the hospital walls. A lady in the city heard about what we did and donated $5,000 worth of shrubbery. Now it's a pretty prime piece of real estate.

Years ago I never would have guessed we'd be able to raise this kind of money or do any of the things we've done for the residents of the Fineson Center. Last year I met President Clinton. Me, Carmine Antonelle! And I carried the torch for the Special Olympics.

This summer, we took sixty kids out for a day of fishing on a big party boat. None of them had ever been fishing before, and they all caught a fish—if you count the same one we kept attaching to everyone's pole. There wasn't anybody who went home without knowing what it feels like to catch a fish. We had a great time, I mean the kind of partying good time that we have at the bar, but without the booze and cigarettes. When we're with the kids, we really don't need that stuff. The kids enjoy everything we do wholeheartedly. It's the world to them. You just feed off of that energy.

I tell anyone thinking about volunteering: you'll get emotionally involved. And when you let yourself become emotionally involved, nothing can bring you down. Our attitude is that nothing can stop us when we're doing something for the kids. Amazing things happen when you give.

Carmine gives away one of the thousands of stuffed animals donated to the Toy Run he organized to benefit nearly 400 mentally and physically challenged children.

SUSANNAH MITCHELL

LAW STUDENT, AGE 25   **NEW ORLEANS, LOUISIANA**

Provides environmental legal research and education

PHOTOGRAPHS BY ELI REED

Going to school at Tulane Law School out here, I've learned a lot about southern Louisiana and its culture. It's such a unique area of the country. Nothing compares to it. Nothing in a book you've read about this place can match it.

Down here people aren't as ready to jump on political issues the way people were in Berkeley, California, where I went to college. But once people learn more and find that volunteering doesn't have to be a burden, they get so involved. Even people in their seventies become dedicated to helping out. I let people know it's okay to commit as much or as little time as they want. I think once people try it, they'll want to come back.

The importance of the work I'm doing at Earthjustice is that we're taking a different approach to fighting environmental abuses. Other groups are fighting to save little sections, a few acres, of the wetlands, like fighting the construction of a race track. We're looking at the preservation of the entire area. We're putting together data that we hope will go toward legislation to make it harder to give all of these companies construction permits. We're being really proactive instead of reactive. Environmental groups usually react to a construction project after it's been started.

Louisiana's coastal ecosystem is disappearing at a faster rate than any other coast in the country because of oil

An alligator suns itself in the Bayou Sauvage, one of many wetlands along the southern Louisiana coast protected by the Earthjustice Legal Defense Fund, Inc., a nonprofit environmental law firm, where Susannah volunteers.

"There are so many different ways you can volunteer," says Susannah. "We hope that the work we do will ensure that our grandchildren can experience these wetlands."

platforms and other development. If you cut down part of a forest in a sustainable manner, it might grow back in several decades. But if you wipe away a portion of the wetlands, you won't see it grow back in your lifetime. It's a different biological makeup.

I've always been intrigued by public interest law—the volunteers of the legal system. They give voice to the indigent. Public interest law isn't pure volunteerism; you are getting paid, just not a lot. But it's still helping people, which is the essence of volunteering—sharing knowledge and skills, bringing something to the table that people haven't experienced before. Helping out other people has definitely become what I want to do in the legal profession. The early volunteer work my parents got me involved in has influenced the direction I'm taking in law school.

I can't fathom being a corporate attorney, representing big business. It's more important for me to know that my skills are helping other people instead of making a hundred thousand dollars a year two years out of school. My impression of corporate lawyers is that they're people helping an industry make more money or protect themselves from state or federal penalties. In the environmental context, they keep a company that dumped chemicals in a swamp from paying its fines.

Earthjustice is a dynamic atmosphere. You have energetic, talented people coming together for the same mission. I did a talk at a Sierra Club meeting, and I liked sharing with people who are interested in an issue, answering their questions; that was definitely an exciting thing for me. I really like interacting, talking to people, and sharing knowledge.

The wetlands work is behind the scenes, but we've done a lot of coalition building with other environmental groups, and it's neat seeing how different the dynamics are. I've met a lot of people

Susannah and Earthjustice staff survey the Bayou Sauvage wetlands, home to several endangered species, with National Forest Service rangers. Two years ago, Susannah initiated Earthjustice's research project on Louisiana wetlands as a volunteer summer clerk.

who have worked for the preservation of wetlands all their lives. They grew up on the bayou. It's great to see residents and citizens getting involved, becoming activists. It's neat to see everyday people dedicate their lives to one issue. If they care about what they're doing, volunteers will always bring this kind of energy.

The political arena down here is very small. You can't go anywhere without running into people who are involved in the government, so you don't feel that your voice gets lost. It's a small community, so you see change happening.

Not having any money is the main challenge we face. Our main adversary is the petroleum industry, and they have more money than I can ever imagine. Our support comes from letter writing; theirs is in the form of cash and campaign contributions. They get more members of Congress on their side.

Every now and then we win because we mobilized people. The National Guard decided not to run tanks through a national forest. It's like David slaying Goliath. Here you are, you don't have anything except people's support, but you force the Army to back down. It's the best feeling.

Volunteering doesn't take as much time as people think. I think I'll always volunteer for some organization. I can't imagine not having enough time for it. But knowing how much time you have is important because if you over-commit, it's easier to give up. My parents are busy professionals, but they take a week out of every summer to put up fences, install water heaters, or paint houses for low-income families.

Once you give volunteering a chance, you'll want to keep doing it. It's about being a productive part of society. You'll start to feel that, and start looking forward to doing it. There's something fulfilling about making progress a little bit at a time.

KEITH MICHAELS

SUBSTANCE ABUSE COUNSELOR, AGE 33 **SANTA MONICA, CALIFORNIA**

Guides blind runners

PHOTOGRAPHS BY JOE BUISSINK

I was hooked before we even took one step, just meeting the athletes with disabilities through the Achilles Track Club.

A lot of people I train with compete, and this organization is not about how fast you are or how many races you've won. It's just people who get together who love to run. And obviously if you're blind, unless you're running on a treadmill, you can't run by yourself. Running has done so much for me in my life—I just decided that guiding a blind runner might be a nice way to give a little bit back to something that's given so much to me.

And certainly the return is a lot greater than I ever expected it to be. There's just really nothing to compare it to. There's nothing like crossing a finish line in a 10K or a marathon with somebody like the two blind runners I guide. It's just an incredible feeling.

Sharlene's been completely blind since birth. She's—she'll kill me if I get this wrong—forty-six or forty-seven years old. She's run thirty marathons—she has an incredible spirit. All she knows how to do is to live life on life's terms without the use of her eyes. She doesn't let being blind get in the way of pursuing her dreams. I really like that about her; that spirit is contagious. You feel like an idiot complaining about the weather, about anything.

I learned to guide, at first, by listening and watching John, one of the other sighted guides.

Keith guides Sharlene Wills on the bike path in Santa Monica. "It's a bit of an art form," says Sharlene, "staying in synch. And Keith is a great guide. He pays attention to what I need, is willing to chat and describe things around us, and can give over his ego to run with me. When he took over to guide me on the second half of the L.A. Marathon, my whole body relaxed. He was there for me."

SPICE ISLANDS
QUICK MEAL
ACHILLES
TRACK
CLUB
PACIFIC BELL
ACHILLES
TRACK
CLUB
adidas

ACHILLES
TRACK CLUB
ULTIMATE

"I was coming back from a fairly long run and ran into a guy I know, John, who started the local Achilles here," Keith says. "When he asked if I wanted to come down and run with them, I said 'sure.' " Here Keith and John touch base before the club's morning run.

Learning how to keep as little tension as possible on the tether, which is the equipment we use to stay connected while we're running.

All the communication is based on two things: verbal communication and chemistry. Sometimes we'll be running and a pretty good amount of time will go by with no verbal communication, but we're always physically communicating. Always. I'll make little, subtle movements in the length of my stride, my breathing pattern, the amount of energy I'm putting out, which Sharlene's now in tune with. That's when it's real nice. That's when it's spiritual.

Another thing that's so cool about Sharlene and Martine, the other blind runner I run with, is that their smiles are so pure. They're not concerned about how they look, I guess, because they don't know what it's like to judge people based on their looks. So their smiles are just huge—these incredibly warm, contagious smiles. I wasn't aware that I was going to learn anything about spirit or attitude when I started running with them. I just showed up, shook some hands, said hello; and week after week, little by little, I became more and more involved. They asked me if I would train to be a guide and I said yeah, absolutely.

I suppose there's a lot of truth to the saying that "The best things in life are free." I go home after showing up at Achilles—on the days when I want to and on the days when I don't want to, when I really don't feel like running seven miles right then—always feeling like I can't wait for next Sunday. Every time.

Life isn't about thinking "What can I get out of it?" Because showing up to get, you show up with a sackful of expectations that are never met. The chances are pretty good you're going to leave feeling empty and unfulfilled. If I approach a situation asking "What can I put into it?" I usually like the results a lot better. So now I ask myself, "What can I bring? What can I show up with and leave here for someone?" And I think that's being spiritually minded. I really believe that you get what you give.

There was a time in my life when I needed a lot of help, and people were there for me. And not only weren't they getting anything back, these were people who didn't know me. And a lot of them weren't getting paid, either—most of them weren't.

Guiding for Achilles has probably done more for me, and given more to me spiritually, than anything ever has in my life. But it's so personal. I'm sure that as moving and life-changing as it's been for me to guide a blind runner to the end of a marathon, to some guy sitting next to me afterward it might not make a damn bit of difference in his life.

For me, life doesn't happen on a couch: I've got to go outside and do things. That's how I figure out what I like and don't like. Sometimes the path leads to the path—it's not the path you're already on; it's the path you're going to.

I'd encourage anybody to do some sort of volunteering in some way. It just makes life more rewarding. You've just got to find out what it is you like to do. Isn't it better to go to bed at night knowing you did something for somebody else, as opposed to putting your head on the pillow thinking, "Look what I got today?"

At this point, if I had to pay some kind of dues or fee to belong to Achilles, I would. Absolutely.

"I like running," Keith says. "That's the bottom line: I'm doing something I love to do, and at the same time I'm helping somebody else do something he or she loves to do. It's just a little more fulfilling because it's not just me, me, me . . . it's us. I like that about it, very much."

ACHILLES
TRACK CLUB
ACHILLES
TRACK CLUB

SCOTT ROSENBERG

ARTIST, AGE 34 NEW YORK, NEW YORK

Founded Art Start to teach at-risk teenagers how to produce film and video

PHOTOGRAPHS BY PAUL FUSCO

My parents were both active in the civil rights movement and were part of the peace movement during the 1960s. My father is a social worker and my mother is a lawyer specializing in domestic violence, so I guess it's not a stretch to say I grew up with a sense of social justice. I remember writing a

letter to Richard Nixon when I was in the second grade, asking him to stop the war in Vietnam.

I never thought I would be as involved with volunteerism as I am now. I bounced around schools in the 1980s, making stops at Brown and Stanford along the way. I finally ended up at NYU, where I attended film school on a Fuji film grant. It was there that I began to realize the impact of media and art as a tool for social change. To me, this is what art is all about—inspiration.

This is something I feel strongly about. We're nearing the 21st century, and there are so many problems in our society, from racism to poverty. We have to do something. We can't sit around. To me, media and art and volunteerism are tools that can be used to reshape our society in a positive way. Art Start is my way of being a rebel, like the young members of the Jewish resistance in Nazi Germany. It's my way of being a warrior for a worthy cause.

Seven years ago I didn't know exactly how I was going to volunteer, but I knew whatever I did, it would involve media and youth. When I formed the Media Works Project in 1993, I wanted it to be a lifelong commitment between the volunteer TV, radio, and film producers and the teens. The kids are really committed and want to help lead new projects and pass on what they've learned. They ask what they can do to help.

Scott (in hat) and his students discuss final editing of "Protect Your Child Against Racism," a public service announcement they've written, directed, and produced as a team.

One student, Margaret Sinclair, told me, "This program raises the velvet rope for us and lets us into the VIP section of the club." It's her way of saying this project is getting them involved with mainstream society, outside of the neighborhoods. But we don't have a "holier-than-thou" or "we're-going-to-help-these-menaces-to-society" attitude about volunteering with kids from the streets. We've got young adults who've been through Riker's Island, but we work with them as equals. We don't just tutor them in media theory and mechanics; we collaborate on real projects. When we meet, workshops aren't like classrooms; they begin like business meetings. We have an agenda we follow. This professionalism is something they appreciate. They're putting their ideas and work out there for the public, and they want it to be the best it can be. They know they must be on time to workshops and meetings, work as a team, help each other out, and tell someone to chill out when they're flipping or just not being positive.

I get at least as much from working with the project as the kids. They've expanded my vision as an artist. They're so clear, direct, and honest when they work together. This is their beauty. They aren't worried

"When I met Scott, I didn't know what to think," says Christopher "Funky" Rolle. "But we both liked rap music, and we vibed off each other. Now I'm at the Manhattan School of Visual Arts, and hopefully, through my art, music, or the screen, I can volunteer my time like Scott does."

about making a faux pas, so their thinking isn't held back. It doesn't matter how many times I've shown a particular image, a different group of kids will see something there that I never considered before. I see something new every time.

It may sound like a cliché, but volunteering with these kids has also helped me to expand as a human being. My outlook on race and diversity has changed. The kids we work with are every color under the sun, from so many different nations and religions, that most people would say, "My, what a diverse group!" But these kids don't see themselves that way. They all share a street culture, a youth culture.

On a visceral level, volunteering is a natural high. You get lifted in the right way when you work with people on something you believe in. It's arduous work, but you come away feeling exhilarated.

I would advise anyone thinking of volunteering to find the thing you love. Find something that you get a kick out of doing, and then find a group of people, a population you aren't familiar with, who you can share it with. It won't be easy, especially in the beginning, but the more work you put into it, the more the experience will be magnified for you.

The Impact of Volunteering

BRIAN O'CONNELL

The caring faces and voices of Keith Michaels, Alison Okinaka, Julie Cotton, and all the other ordinary extraordinary volunteers pictured in these pages are multiplied millions of times every day by a great many people like them who care and do something about it.

As a result, volunteers achieve a stunning impact on an almost endless number of problems and dreams. The composite of all their individual acts of kindness and courage moves mountains of pain, hopelessness, neglect, and indifference and, with each success, provides hope and examples for all the rest of us.

I don't want to take the slightest chance that these glorious truths about the good that volunteers do will be lost or diluted in abstract praise, so let me be very precise about the impact.

In just the past twenty years, volunteers have broken through centuries of institutional indifference to the needs of the dying, and as a result of their noble crusade, almost every community today already has hospice services to provide relief to the terminally ill and their families.

In very recent times, volunteers' passion, courage, and tenacity have forced the nation and every region in it to realize that we must preserve for future generations our precious resources of water, air, and land. That ethic and practice have now spread to every form of local and national asset including wetlands, forests, farmland, and historic buildings and districts.

Volunteers stood up and were counted for common decency and adequate services for retarded children, and with those breakthroughs showed the way to many others who then dared to do the same for cerebral palsy, autism, learning disabilities, and hundreds of other problems we hadn't even heard of twenty years ago.

With the establishment and growth of Alcoholics Anonymous, volunteers pioneered a model of mutual assistance that today extends to almost every serious personal problem. In almost every community there's a group of people who have weathered the storm and are reaching out to others newly faced with such threatening crises as the death of a child, mastectomy, depression, stroke, or physical abuse.

Volunteers sang "we are not afraid," though of course they were—but with each new volunteer recruited to the crusade, their courage, confidence, and power grew, and then when their vast army sang and believed "we shall overcome," they did.

The Civil Rights Movement then spread to every disenfranchised and under-represented group including women, physically disabled, Native Americans, Hispanics, and so many more.

A few volunteers, at first mostly parents and students, believed they could do something about drunk driving, but despite the escalating ravages, most of us didn't think they would succeed. Thank God they did.

With the increasing evidence of the power of ordinary people, more individuals realized that maybe—just maybe—they could also change public policies and behavior about smoking, and look what they've done.

Dealing with community problems was one thing, but some issues defied organization or were even off-limits for reasons of national security. However, some people believed that matters such as control of nuclear power were linked to survival, so volunteers stepped in, at their peril, to reduce our peril.

Volunteers even began to take peace into their territory with people-to-people understanding as a fundamental step to reduce international tensions and build tolerance and friendship.

And all the time a healthy number of people served all of us by promoting the importance and availability of arts and cultural opportunities as central aspects of a civilized society. One of the great waves of voluntary activity and impact has involved community theater, dance, and music to provide opportunities for creativity and enjoyment of it.

The list goes on almost endlessly including major advances in day care, consumer advocacy, population control, conflict resolution, ethnic museums, early infant care, independent living for the elderly, teen pregnancy prevention, substance abuse prevention and treatment, job training, and so very much more.

We are also learning a great deal more about the astounding variety of causes served and of the ways volunteers serve them. Here's a very small sampling of all that Americans care about:

Neighborhood Improvement, Overseas Relief, Education, Conservation and Preservation, Public Broadcasting, Animal Rights, Community Arts, Job Training, Illiteracy, Toxic Waste, Garden Clubs, Endangered Species, Learning Disabilities, Hospitals, Blood Banks, Support Groups, Legal Aid, Public Interest Law, Crime Prevention, Homebound Employment, Food Banks, Tenant Rights, Homelessness, Disaster Preparedness, Camping, Religious Congregations, Civil Rights, Day Care, Peer Counseling, International Exchange, Voter Registration, Scientific Exploration, and on and on and on.

Studies show that Americans believe they have an obligation to be involved and that they are willing to do so. But this research also indicates that people don't know what's expected of them in the fulfillment of their community service and that, with guidance, they will strive to contribute their fair share. To provide that guidance and to reflect and build on the more than 23 million Americans who already volunteer five or more hours a week, INDEPENDENT SECTOR launched its "Give Five" program. The organization acknowledges that the tithers are still the true leaders of our caring society but suggests that all of us should give at least five hours a week and 5 percent of our income to the causes we care about.

John W. Gardner, my co-founder at INDEPENDENT SECTOR, says that "almost every major social breakthrough in America has originated in this voluntary sector." He goes on that "if volunteers and voluntary organizations were to disappear from our national life, we would be less distinctly American. The sector enhances our creativity, enlivens our communities, nurtures individual responsibility, stirs life at the grassroots, and reminds us that we were born free. Its vitality is rooted in good soil—civic pride, compassion, a philanthropic tradition, a strong problem-solving impulse, a sense of individual responsibility, and an irrepressible commitment to the great shared task of improving our life together."

When most of us think about the impact of volunteering, we quite naturally focus on the benefits for the people and causes served. However, there are other important and encouraging consequences that add greatly to the good that is achieved when so many people are engaged in doing so many good things.

Research now makes clear that when individuals make an effort for the public good, not only are others helped, but something special happens for the giver too. Volunteers feel good about themselves and gain a significant degree of personal satisfaction and fulfillment.

Also, when so many active and thoughtful people are part of a community, there is greater respect for community, greater awareness of shared hopes, and a higher level of civility and acts of kindness.

Finally, when almost one out of two Americans regularly helps each other to improve our shared condition, the country as a whole takes on a spirit of compassion, comradeship, and confidence. In essence, when you add up all the impacts of volunteering, everybody wins.

In the most fundamental ways, 100 million volunteers make America a participatory and successful nation.

KATHERINE PENER

COUNTY ELECTIONS COORDINATOR, AGE 84 **MIAMI BEACH, FLORIDA**

Counsels breast cancer patients after surgery

PHOTOGRAPHS BY ED KASHI

I'm a breast cancer survivor, and I help women who've had surgery for breast cancer. I've volunteered for the Reach to Recovery program for twenty-two years.

As I train volunteers for the program, I always ask myself, "How can I teach the spirit of volunteerism?" That's when you volunteer even when you don't feel good, when you're sick. I volunteer on my birthdays; I volunteered on the day my brother died. It's not something you do when it's convenient, and you don't cancel when you have an appointment at the beauty parlor. It's being dedicated to your cause and to the people you help.

I feel strongly about this because volunteering has kept me alive. The great feeling I have when I help cancer patients keeps me physically and mentally well. I even think volunteering helps your immune system. And it's spiritual. The Jewish people have a word for doing a good deed; it's called a "mitzvah." When you do that, there's an angel looking over you, taking care of you. My husband says I must have a million of them up there looking after me. Retired people who just sit around and play cards and eat lunch and shop—they start to complain about life. Life loses its meaning.

People say I don't look like I'm in my eighties. Well, I agree. I'll work at the county for six hours, then visit the doctors' offices and see patients, and then make a house call and not get home until ten p.m. I'll still be charged because my heart's in it, my brain's alive and thinking. The patients inspire me. I keep cards on all my patients so I can keep in touch. They tell me, "You saved my life; you gave me hope," and that rejuvenates me.

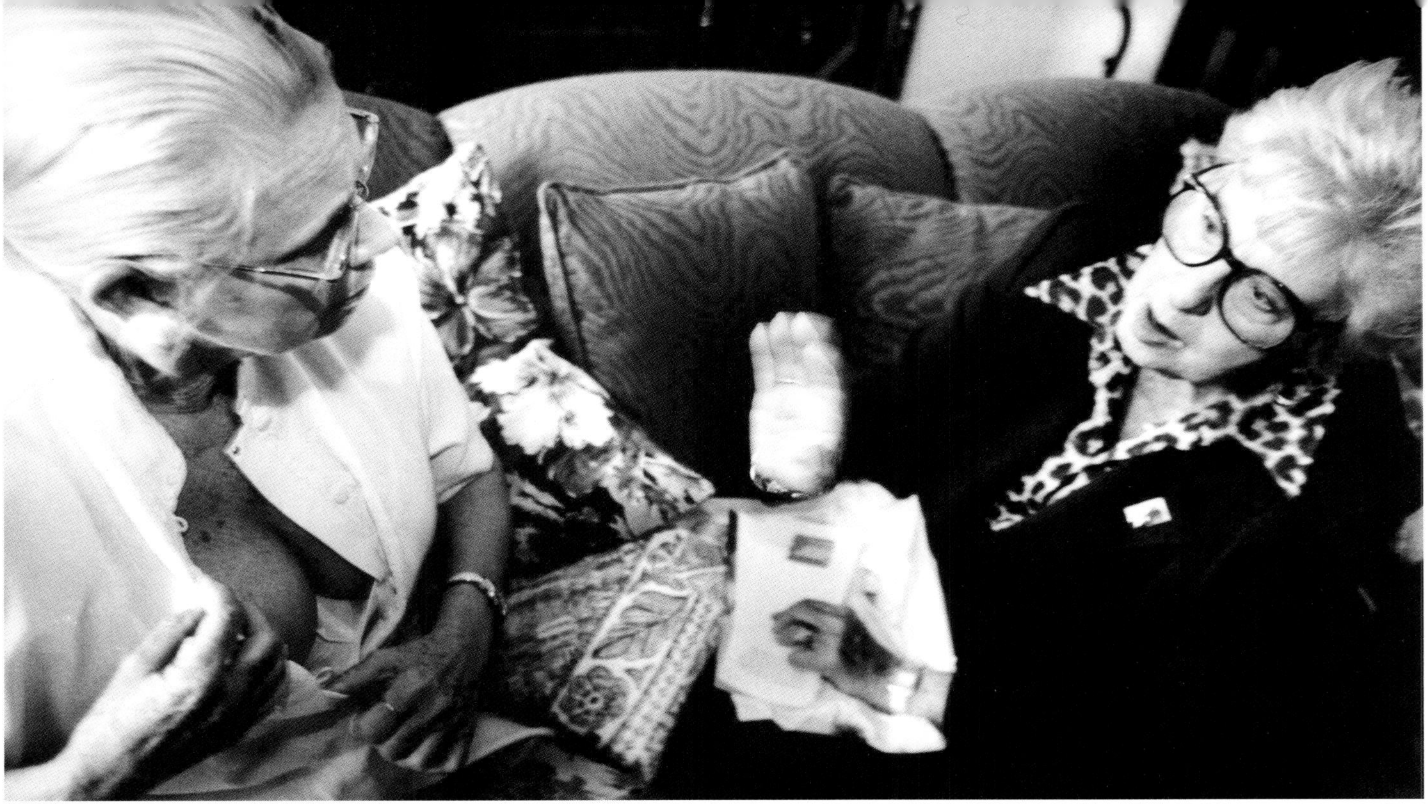

“My first priority is the patients,” says Katherine (right), with Kay Doxey after Kay’s bilateral mastectomy. “If they lost some hair because of chemotherapy, we look for a wig together. If they feel alone, then I’m a friend. If they fear their fella will be concerned, I tell them my husband loved me more after my surgery, because I was alive and he could have lost me.”

"Katherine has a huge commitment to breast cancer survivors," says Kay, of Katherine's several visits to her home after surgery. "It's so important to form a network with people who've experienced breast cancer. Nobody understands like they do."

My patients live. They live, they are happy, and they are grateful.

When people are told they have cancer, they think, "I'm going to die." I thought I was going to die. My mother and aunts died of cancer. So thank God I had a loving husband and a job to go back to—that was my saving grace. At the time of my mastectomy I was an assistant principal in the New York City public school system. I went back to work on St. Patrick's Day and wore a prosthesis, and I had the chutzpah to wear a sleeveless green sweater. All the teachers' eyes were on me. They knew I had had a radical mastectomy, and they wanted to see if they could tell. The kids were fine, but not the adults.

I learned that having cancer changes the way people think about you. I applied to be the head principal of an elementary school, but I was refused by the chair of the school board because I had had a mastectomy. She said I was too great a risk. Cancer was a dirty word back then; it still is. I was seen as sick and feeble. But here I am. I outlived her. So I tell my patients to get out and get back to work. That's the road to recovery, getting back to a normal life.

Reach to Recovery works because all the volunteers helping women through the trauma of breast cancer and surgery have been there themselves. Seeing the volunteers, women know they can beat this. It's critical that women see a survivor. A patient's eyes light up when I say it's been twenty-nine years since I had my operation.

Now with HMOs, we have "drive-by mastectomies"—patients are in and out in twenty-three hours—they're not hospitalized long enough to make a hospital call. So now we do house calls and see women in their doctors' offices before surgery. It doesn't matter where we meet. What matters is the woman-to-woman contact. We don't give medical advice; we give woman-to-woman advice. We let them know what to expect. We know all those little personal things, so we can reassure them and say, "I had the same thing. It's routine."

The Reach to Recovery program was founded in 1952 by Therese Lasa, a breast cancer survivor. Like others before her, she had no one to turn to during that ordeal. The American Cancer Society adopted the program the same year I had my surgery, in 1969. I read about the program in the *New York Post* and asked my doctor, "Shouldn't I have one of these visitors?" The doctor said, "What do you need them for?" That feeling of being alone I will never forget. I felt so hopeless.

The first time I cried was when I was given that pink prosthesis by the doctors. The thought that

I would have to wear this for the rest of my life was almost too much. We are such a breast-oriented society; for a woman to lose her breasts threatens her womanhood. Now as a volunteer, I understand the great need for helping a woman get through that and then get back her self-esteem.

People need tremendous support to go through the operation, but going through the chemotherapy is even worse. It's a draining, dangerous procedure, one of the reasons women are afraid to be checked out for breast cancer. It's tough on a woman to lose her hair and eyebrows. That's why we have cosmeticians who meet with the women, give them free wigs and makeup, and teach them how to feel beautiful again. When you look better, you feel better.

I guarantee anyone who volunteers will feel better emotionally, physically, and psychologically. I don't care who you are or what you do. The people I know who volunteer have smiles on their faces. The hours they give are worth more to them than any money they could ever receive.

You don't have to have gone through what the people you help have gone through. You just need to give your time, that's all. Don't worry about whether you can do it or not. Get out of the house and help out. You help a human being, and that person is going to be grateful. You'll be proud of yourself, and your family will be so proud of what you do.

When I go to a woman's home after surgery and see her in all that pain, I make sure to bring in a positive attitude. I want to let her know that she will go back to work, that she will be a loving wife again. If she's divorced, I let her know she'll look great and will get out and meet people again. I hope when I visit I'll be an inspiration.

JULIE COTTON

LAB RESEARCHER, AGE 35 **FORT COLLINS, COLORADO**

Trains search and rescue dogs

PHOTOGRAPHS BY JOHN EISELE

The volunteer work I do can be emotional. Last year a sheriff was killed by two bank robbers, but they got away on foot into a nearby forest and presumably into one tiny mountain town. They were terrified. This was the kind of town that left the front doors open, and now people were keeping their kids inside.

The FBI was called in; they thought the couple may have died from exposure and asked us to come in on a second search of the mountain area. We brought in three dog teams. In fifty minutes we found them: the robbers had killed themselves just one mile from the vehicle. This couple had been on a killing spree across the country and had a sticker for each state they'd been through. It was intense, but a relief, when we let the news out that their bodies had been found. Church bells rang out in the town when the news hit.

There's a professionalism we have to have for this kind of volunteer work. We're working with local, state, and federal law enforcement officials, so the attitude that "I'm just a volunteer and don't have to be that good" just doesn't cut it. I've been told by police officers that we have professional training on par with their own.

I live for search and rescue, and I go to work to support my volunteer habit. I've been doing this since 1986, and people I know through Larimer County Search and Rescue, and Search and Rescue Dogs of Colorado, have become like my family.

Two years ago, I was at a rescue team conference in central Colorado when we were called about a

Tassie, an Australian Cattle dog, leads Julie to two Boy Scouts buried in snow. Nine scouts volunteered to be buried for this search and rescue avalanche training at Cameron Pass, Colorado.

search in Wyoming for a missing four-year-old girl. At the time, she had been lost for four hours in a national forest. We arrived at noon the next day, so now she's been missing for twelve hours. Her scent was heavy around Beaver Pond, and in situations like these you get a horrible, sinking feeling. Most of the time you can separate yourself emotionally and focus 100 percent on your job, but not always. We were ready to go out on the water when we heard from my husband, Bill. He had stopped for a break and just listened to the wind. He heard a noise and found her. She was two miles from camp and had gone through some rough terrain. She had been missing for twenty hours. There were screams of joy and jumping up and down when we heard he found

After "finding her human," Tassie gets her reward toy from Julie, who trains her dogs to circle where the scent is strongest and bark loudly until the search and rescue team shows up.

her. Five minutes after they picked her up, a snow blizzard hit and it was a total white-out. You can't follow a scent in a blizzard.

You have to keep an open mind, and stay hopeful, but sometimes you'll find a dead body. Usually a search is over in four hours, but when it goes to twelve hours and you don't find anyone—particularly with kids—the pressure is on, and it gets incredibly stressful.

On the tenth anniversary of my marriage, we were home celebrating and were paged with the report that a child was lost in Rocky Mountain National Park. It was big news, and we heard about it on the radio on the drive there. As we got out, we passed kids who recognized us from an elementary school presentation we did a few weeks before. They asked me if I was going to save their sister. Normally, you don't know the people you're searching for. This was a night mission, around midnight, and we could hear other teams out there and see their lights. You know something's wrong, because you know a lost child should be hearing and seeing this, too. It makes your stomach turn. By daybreak a dog had found her body.

For one search on a fourteen-thousand-foot mountain, it made more sense to do a 'copter pick-up for this injured person than hike for eight hours, but the 'copter lost its balance and crashed into the mountain. The pilot and flight nurse were killed. From then on I saw people who do this differently: we are risking our lives. I had to reevaluate what I do. I never thought about quitting, but reality hit me and I wasn't romanticizing it anymore. It made me more dedicated.

I get emotional now when I watch search-and-rescue missions on the news. I think what neat people those are and how glad I am they're out there. Then I realize, "I do this!" When I started it was a personal challenge; it was personal growth. I was just an outdoors person who did a lot of hiking and backpacking. I didn't know how to use a map and compass, or how to climb or rappel down a mountain—I had to learn all that. Now people see me as some intense person who knows everything about dogs and about search and rescue. But I'm still constantly learning.

Search and rescue work has brought my husband out of his shell. He was a shy guy, and now he's developed leadership potential. I'm more confident now, too. It's great watching people progress.

It's hard to think about this, but I've lost track of the people I've found. Helping people is why I do this, even though most of our time is spent in training, not in real rescues. But if not for that personal contact, finding people who need help, I might not spend so much time training.

If you volunteer, you have to pick something you're going to have time to do. Search and rescue is not for someone who has limited time. You have to train and keep your skills up. But there are so many ways to volunteer; you can always find something you have time for. Doing ninety hours a year is fine if you're dedicated. I do that in a month, but that's because it's my passion. You're volunteering in your free time, so it has to be what you really enjoy. Don't do it because you think you're supposed to. I don't understand the idea of community service as a punishment when it's assigned by a judge. I have a problem with that. It should be a reward or a hobby.

Everyone has talents. You have to find out what yours are and then volunteer with that. And you have to feel personal satisfaction from helping others. We tell people if they're doing this for the "glory" to go elsewhere. Volunteer for yourself, not to get any sort of external reward from other people.

As for me, I grew up with animals. I'm close to dogs and like spending time with them. I didn't get my own dogs with the intent to make them search dogs. They're pets first. Zephyr was five months old and afraid of the world when I brought him home from the shelter. I think he was abused because he ducks when you raise your hand. He had to be forced to do anything, but his confidence really soared when he started rescuing people. He doesn't spook as much now. He loves to be outdoors. The dogs are happy when they find their person—and everyone around them is telling them how wonderful they are. It's positive reinforcement, they feel great, and their behavior changes.

People aren't so different.

Zephyr, one of Julie's search and rescue dogs, digs out Tyler Thomas, in this avalanche training session. "We look for people who like to be outdoors and can work easily with others," says Julie of the volunteers who help her.

JIM HUMPHREY

RETIRED BUILDING INSPECTOR, AGE 60 **BATTLE CREEK, MICHIGAN**

Counsels survivors of domestic violence

PHOTOGRAPHS BY ELAINE LITTLE

Before I started volunteering here, my thoughts were, "Why would a woman go back to a man who beats on her?" I learned there are many reasons why that never did cross my mind. There is the honeymoon period, where the man promises to change, brings flowers and candy and says, "Honey, this will never happen again." And they love this person and want to believe it. Then there's economics, threats to kill the children, threats to have the kids taken away. And women believe that this will happen if they leave.

You read in the paper, you hear in the news, a man burned himself, wife and daughters, set the house on fire, because he was going through a divorce and didn't want to lose anything. Women in severely abusive situations see this on the news and fear this will happen to them.

I knew what crisis counseling was before I started volunteering with S.A.F.E. Place. I had women friends who were counseling volunteers. And I used to do a lot of talking, especially with people who were going through problems. Whenever you're talking and listening, you're counseling. A friend saw an article about S.A.F.E. Place needing help and suggested I see about lending a hand. There are men who do this kind of volunteering. A few, anyway.

I talked to the director four years ago, and she thought I would be good with the phone lines, and maybe the intake and crisis counseling. I've always had a gift for listening. I'm not judgmental. I think I have the wisdom to listen and talk in a helping way.

The first six weeks at S.A.F.E. Place was just learning the operation and going through forty-five hours of training. Then it was constant counseling

"I think I was gifted for counseling," says Jim, here listening to a client during a support group meeting. "I'm a people person. And I'm not judgmental." He's currently the only male volunteer with S.A.F.E. Place, a domestic violence shelter and crisis intervention center in Battle Creek, Michigan.

"I don't see people get worse," says Jim, assisting two professional counselors in a support group meeting in the shelter's living room. "Most get better, because this is time away from the negative environment that brought them here."

and intakes. When the clients come in, we sit down and talk to them, go through lots of paperwork, and ask them what went on in their lives to bring them here.

Sometimes a women has a problem with a male crisis counselor. I was warned about that when I started. They told me that calls would come in where the woman may hang up if a man answers the phone. And that did happen. I can understand why some women do that. It's more comfortable talking to another woman when issues like sexual abuse come up. If there's a problem like that, I just hand the phone over to one of the women counselors.

With face-to-face counseling, some women appreciate talking to a man because they can get the man's point of view—an open-minded point of view. All men are not bad. That's what I tell the women. I've also been told it's good to have a man at the shelter because it's a positive role model for the children staying there.

The greatest rewards I have received while here are two cards from two women thanking me for the help I gave them. They stayed for a while and

Jim keeps an eye on both residents' and other volunteers' kids whenever he's at the shelter. Along with offering emotional support, counselors like Jim are trained to teach clients parenting and discipline skills.

then moved on. Months later I got cards thanking me for being there. When you know you can help somebody and point them in a better direction, it's so rewarding. It lets you know there are people out there who appreciate what you do.

At first I wondered if a volunteer could help a person's life get better. But I'm a positive person. I knew there would be some way I could help. Communal living is hard for many people. The women here are leaving an environment that was rough and coming into one where everyone is a stranger. I realized part of my job was just to make people feel comfortable.

The first night they come in, most battered women are nervous. They just left a bad situation, and they're usually exhausted. It takes a couple of days before they open up and meet other clients and talk. It can take a week before they smile.

When someone comes in, really distraught and just about losing it, it's hard to find the right words to say. What can you say to a woman who just left a man who beat her up bad or is trying to kill her? Most of the time I just sit and listen. If you've had bad problems, all anyone can tell you is that things will get better. So I search for the right words. I try to provide empathy.

To see how these women move on and find an apartment, trying to make a change, is inspiring. And believe me it is a struggle for them. Some of their biggest fears are about getting out on their own.

Volunteering is great because it puts me in a different environment. I had friends and hang-outs through work, but you lose all of that when you retire. Volunteering has broadened my horizons. I've made new friends. Every day is a new day.

Everyone should give volunteering a try. You'll be surprised by what you have to offer. It only takes one or two hours a week to make a difference. Any nonprofit can use the help. Do something.

PATRICIA ESPARZA

PUBLIC HOUSING ADMINISTRATOR, AGE 36 **EL PASO, TEXAS**

Founder and director of Las Mariposas, a dance troupe for young girls

PHOTOGRAPHS BY WILLIAM MERCER MCLEOD

When I was ten, I was a translator for my mother and her friends, who didn't speak English. They called me the little social worker, *la trabajadorita social*. So volunteering is part of my day-to-day life. It's part of my personality. With Mariposas, I realize how much need is out there. I realize how much one person can change things when they give without expecting anything back.

Seeing the girls blossom is why I do this. Some don't talk when they join. Witnessing them open up gives me goose bumps.

It's not easy at first. Girls who are twelve and thirteen have such attitude. When I ask them what they want out of life, they say, *¿para qué?* which means, "what for?" They don't believe anything good is going to happen in their lives. But once they're in the group, they start to realize their potential. They freak out when they see themselves in the makeup and the outfits, and they hear the applause of the audience. They say, "Aw, man, I kicked butt! My Mom came to see this and I actually did good!"

It gives me a high. Also, my paid job is so stressful, the music and choreographing dance relax me.

Nine years ago, my daughters told me I cared more about my job than about them. I wanted to start something with them we could both enjoy. We started dancing, practicing on a basketball blacktop near my grandmother's house. We didn't have a name back then. Then other little girls started coming over to watch my four girls. We invited those little girls to join in. Their mothers came and watched too. I never thought it would grow into this.

After one of my daughters, Jennifer, had a school project on butterflies, tracking their development from caterpillar to chrysalis to butterfly, we called ourselves Las Mariposas. It's all about development. Change within yourself.

The group has grown since then. Girls come and go, with a steady base of about forty girls. The growth includes the community because the parents are a part of it. The troupe has grown as far as dancing and numbers, but one of the most beautiful things is that a lot of the mothers have found support from each other. In Spanish we say, *carnalismo,* which means brotherhood, but in this case it's sisterhood.

In Mariposas, the parents have to come to the parenting meetings, or their children cannot perform with the troupe. You need to teach responsibility.

"I can relate to these girls, and they know where I'm coming from," says Pat, who was the mother of three at age nineteen. "The girls have a lot of questions, and they know when you're being honest."

"I always loved to dance," says Pat, teaching young members of Las Mariposas, a modern dance troupe she founded for at-risk girls in El Paso, Texas. "I cleaned the restrooms where my mother worked to earn enough to pay for my dance classes and costumes."

Nothing is free in life. I'm not asking for money. I ask for two hours of their time, and I don't think that's asking too much. Their children don't want to hear from me that they are doing good, they want to hear it from their parents. That's why they must be involved.

I provide parenting courses that I was trained to do and bring in social workers and counselors. I've brought in lawyers to talk about family law. I'm blessed with the job I have because I can do a lot of referrals to the proper city agencies. It's a relaxed setting. It's their turf, their barrio.

I had my first daughter when I was seventeen and was a mother of three by nineteen. I got my degree in 1988 in social work. My educational and social backgrounds have given me sensitivity when approaching the girls and their mothers. I help in a humble way. Other people blow them off because they don't speak English, but these women bring with them so many values and ethics from Mexico.

"My grandmother called me *gusanito*, the little worm, because I would move around so much," says Pat. "Now I have my own *gusanitos* to look after."

I'll be honest: I don't concentrate on how other people view the group. I focus on the dancing and forget about everything else. I feel extreme contentment doing this. I'm getting a lot back. We've gotten some recognition, but I don't care. I do this because it really gives me a high. There have been times when I was going to cut back on the time I put in, but I can't. I can't sit at home on weekends. I thank God for the energy I have. I'll keep going as long as God keeps giving me the energy.

The closest people around me volunteer. I think it's primarily because we had a need. We grew up in such poor neighborhoods, we didn't have our own stuff, we had to share. We had to help one another.

Do you really want to volunteer? If you say, "Well, yeah, but . . . ," then you want to volunteer for the wrong reasons. Why do you want to be there? Do you want to share something? Do you want to contribute? I hear people say, "I started volunteering for these at-risk kids last month but I quit, because they have no hope." You can't expect to change anything overnight. Do it because it gives you something.

I get my drive in life from my grandmother. Grandma's philosophy was that in order for you to consider yourself a part of the human race, you have to give to it. She would say the best resource we have is people, not money. It is the human element that will make a strong community and world. She had a saying, *un granito de arena,* a grain of sand—that's the literal translation, but it means you need to plant the seed.

JOHN GATUS

RETIRED STEAM FITTER, AGE 58 **OMAHA, NEBRASKA**

Supervises an anti-gang street patrol

PHOTOGRAPHS BY ALEX WEBB

I've been with MAD DADS since its inception in 1989. That was the year my stepson was killed.

We're a national organization of men dedicated to ending street violence. We do a lot of different things, but basically we reach out to young people. In every community, young people seem to be in a rut. But this is especially true in the black community, where they're killing each other.

MAD DADS is my first volunteer effort. My stepson, Windell, was murdered by a gang member in downtown Omaha—maybe he said the wrong thing or looked at someone the wrong way, but a young man walked up to him and put a gun in his mouth and pulled the trigger. Windell was nineteen; the young man who pulled the trigger was sixteen.

I attended the funeral feeling like all hope was gone for the younger generation. I felt like somewhere something went wrong with our community

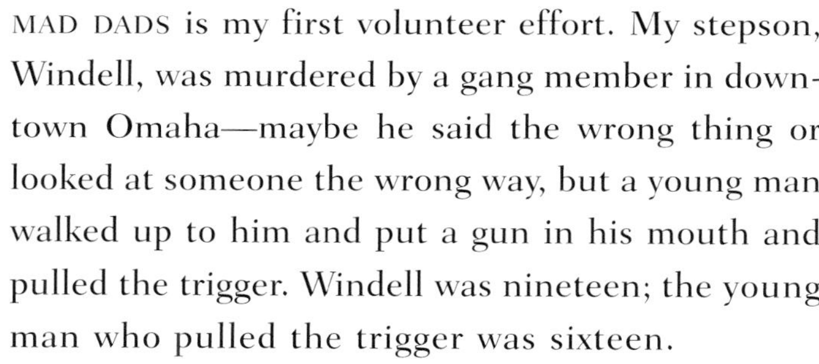

"On cold nights we stop where teenagers hang out, just to let people know we're out here," says John, greeting LaShanda Collier near midnight at Big Jim's Convenience Store.

and nothing could be done. But right after Windell's funeral, I heard about an organization of men who wanted to do something to end violence. This was a group of men, like me, whose sons and grandsons and nephews were dealing with the gangs and drug problems.

I knew that working with the young men who were in gangs was the only way to help things get better. And I knew if I didn't join, I would lose all hope. We had a gang problem, but the police and the city were in denial about it. People think that because this is the Midwest, we don't have the problems an L.A. or a New York City has. But the year my stepson was killed, there were seven other young deaths related to gangs. After that year, people finally opened their eyes.

"We pray every night before we leave for patrol," says John, with Steve Gregory at the MAD DADS Information Center. "We don't fear the kids out there, but we fear what could happen."

When I first started working with MAD DADS, I was focused on the gangs because of Windell. I wanted to see for myself the kids who were caught up in gangs. I wanted to talk to them. I wanted to find out what was wrong with these young men. I soon realized that a lot of the violence was due to drugs. Once they start dealing, gangs fight over turf. I was told my stepson was a "wannabe," that he wasn't in a gang but had friends who were, and he hung out with them at a family park. I can't believe it became the scene of an execution.

You could say I was obsessed with the gang problem. But not in a vengeful way. The founder of MAD DADS, John Foster, had a son who came home from school one day really beat up. He was a "mad dad" at the time. He called other men his age who were experiencing the same anger and held a meeting with clergy that led to forming the group. I was at that first meeting, but I never felt rage. When Windell was killed, I was hurt. I was hurt bad, and I wanted to do something that would make a real change. I had no idea of the drug trade when I started out. None of us did. We painted over graffiti, went to schools and told kids to stay away from gangs, but we weren't really confronting the problem.

So we started the Street Patrol. We went out at night, a bunch of middle-aged men—and we probably looked funny, out of place, out of touch. There was some fear, too.

A lot of the older guys didn't want to come face to face with gang members who carried knives or guns, but those of us who were not afraid had to do it. We don't carry weapons; the only weapon we have is our conversation. We didn't know what we were going to run into.

"There's a certain amount of courage you need to do this," says John. "That's volunteering. You have to have understanding, and you have to want to help no matter what the consequences."

Volunteer work brings real change, change you can be a part of, change you can see with your own eyes. You don't need politicians or the police to tell you things are better. You can see it and feel it for yourself, and know you were a part of it. One guy who was a gang leader works with young people now. And we have a gun buy-back

program. A year ago we went to the city and businesses and raised $50,000 and then bought back guns—$50 a gun. We collected almost one thousand and melted them all down. Now that felt good.

You know what else feels good? We'll drive out and walk our patrol, and when we see young people, we'll get out and talk to them. We tell them who we are and ask them what can we do to help them out. They usually need jobs, so we refer them to Job Corps or the NAACP. Everyone has a different problem—sometimes it's school, sometimes it's parents or other gangs. So over the years, I've learned. And the gang problem isn't what it used to be in Omaha. There was only one killing last summer.

The Patrol has changed my life. Although I've retired, I do something that's really meaningful to me. I spend most of my time with MAD DADS, three to four hours every day in the office, doing paperwork and talking with people who call in and need help. We've done mentoring at every grade school, high school, and college in Omaha.

I never get tired of volunteering. It's not like a job where you punch in, do your time, and then go home. It's part of my life. We have uniforms and a name. There's real pride involved. We're part of the community, and we like being recognized as positive black men.

NADIA BEN-YOUSSEF

STUDENT, AGE 13 **SIDNEY, MONTANA**

Writes poetry and sings for older people

PHOTOGRAPHS BY JOHN EISELE

Sharing is part of my life. It's not a separate part of my life. It's me. Even when I was little it just dawned on me one day that sharing is what I'm here for.

If you know you were made to write or paint or do something special, you have your whole life ahead of you to do it. Sharing and singing, for me, is a gift. Everyone has a gift; you just need to realize it before you can share it. I discovered mine at a young age. If I didn't know until I was fifty, it would be okay, but it would have been with me all that time.

Time is life. When you think about life, there's only so much time. But volunteering, giving of yourself, is not giving up time. It's finding something new. So there's nothing to lose. Life was made for giving others love. That's the only way to live.

I've been singing and performing poetry since I was six years old. I guess I've volunteered since I was eight. My singing is a cappella; I don't sing with music. My singing and poetry are the same thing. I used to sing for my mother's friends, and then I started singing for fund-raisers put on by church groups, women's clubs, the Lions Club, and stuff like that.

My dad travels a lot. He's part of many Arab and medical associations. So I've been to Morocco and I sang there. I performed for the Arab American Medical Association in Washington, D.C. I sang at Concordia College in Minnesota when I was nine. That was the biggest audience that I had ever performed in front of. More than two thousand students, teachers, and people were there. That was wild. It was a convention called Who Cares For Our Children? I was nervous because it was the most people I've ever seen in one place, but I

"I discovered at a young age that I want to give, share, and make people happy for the rest of my life." Here, Nadia sings to residents of the Sidney Health Center's nursing home.

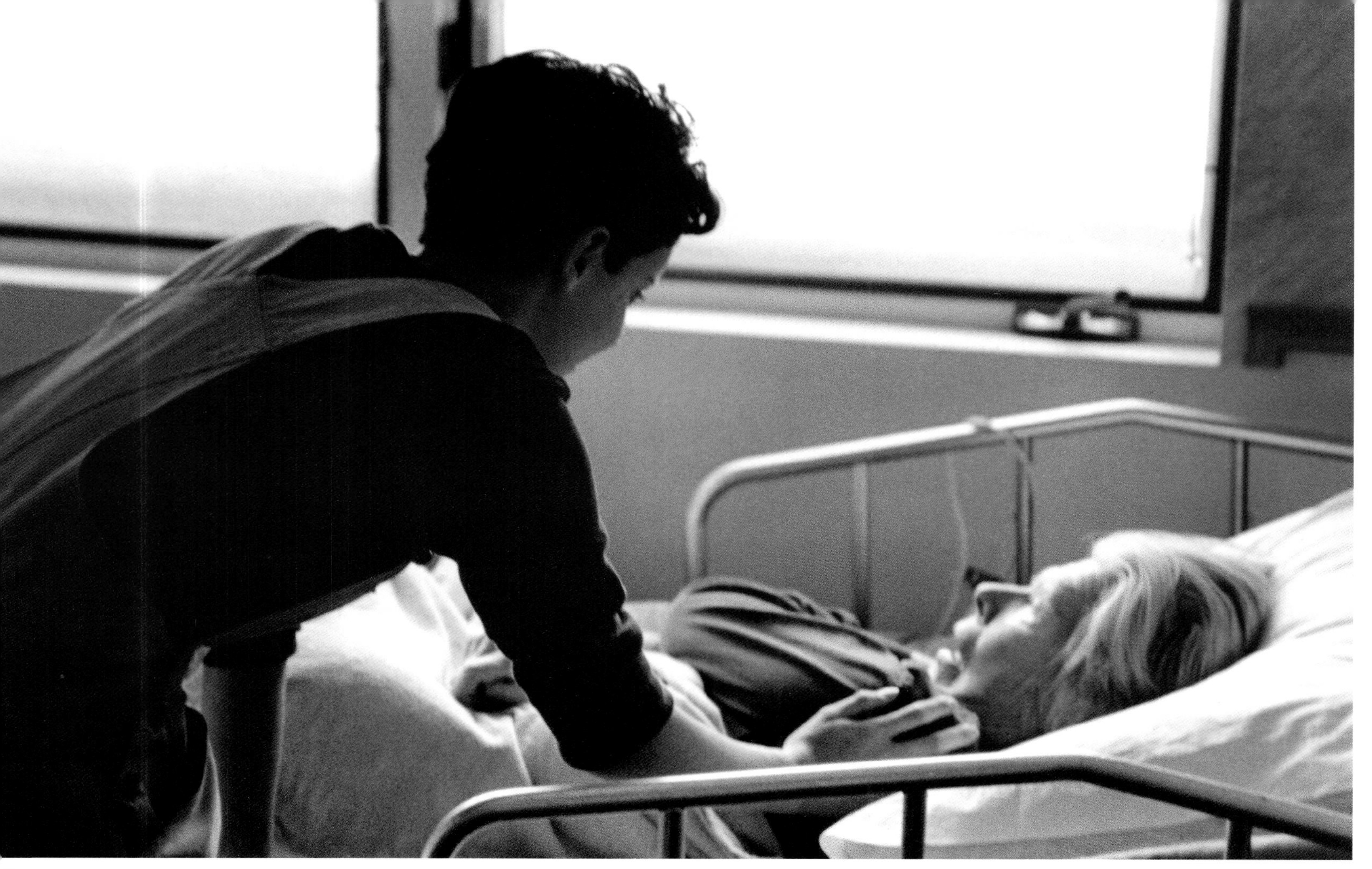

"Older people understand my music the best," says Nadia, with Annie Smith at the Sidney Health Center in Sidney, Montana. "They understand life because they have fulfilled it, I guess."

wasn't very self-conscious. I just went up there and sang. Afterward, the director of the college knelt down, because I was kind of short, and told me I'll have a scholarship in nine years.

I have three books of poetry and songs. A fourth is in production. I donate all of the money from the books to children's charities. Money from my first book went to a school for deaf and blind kids in Great Falls, Montana, and to the Lions Club. They did a campaign called Sight First to help the blind. Money from the second book went to Home on the Range, a shelter for abused children, and to the Feed The Children fund for orphans in Bosnia.

Two years ago I sang at St. Jude's Children's Research Hospital for children with cancer in Memphis, Tennessee. That was wonderful. I got to hand out gifts to the children. Later my mom and I saw a story about it on TV, a special on St. Jude's, and I decided that's where the money from my next book would go.

When I sing for people, sometimes they get tears in their eyes. Sometimes they smile. Sometimes they look at me before I sing like, "I'm not going to listen to some eight-year-old." But then after I'm done, they're ready to give hugs. They're happy, I guess.

I visit people at a local nursing home. I do the women's hair, I do their nails, and they ask me to come by on Sundays and perform for them. And I do. There's no microphone and no musical accompaniment. I also sing for home-bound hospice patients. I visit them and talk and sing for them. I guess that's what's really fulfilling to me, when I sing to someone who is dying, someone who is really sick, and who isn't aware of much of what's happening, but when I'm done there's a smile on that person's face.

I'm more comfortable singing for old people. They've gone through a lot of life. They have experience. They understand my music more than people my age. They understand life because they have fulfilled it, I guess.

I sing a lot about death and the afterlife. I sing about the unknown and the beauty of life and the beauty of death. It's not disturbing to me. It's really peaceful when I'm done singing. I'm not doing anything big. I'm just being there. Why should I be disturbed? People who are dying know where they're going and I know where they're going. It's not like I'm singing to someone who is dying. I'm singing to someone who is getting ready to live again.

I get my perspective from within. I guess it's from God. Sometimes I sing and I don't know where it came from. It doesn't make sense until it comes out of my mouth. Words just flow out. I don't have to write them down sometimes.

I find that everyone needs love, everyone can give love, and that love is what everyone wants. That's a really important lesson to me. Making someone happy makes you happy, and they go on and make others happy and it's like a chain. Love is a chain of giving. You change when you get older, but love is ageless. Love is the same when you are 7, 13, or 102.

To think that one person doesn't make a difference is totally backwards. Volunteering and giving starts with one person. To think you don't have time is ridiculous. Every day you have twenty-four hours. Just smiling is something you can do. Volunteering doesn't take effort. It's something you can do unconsciously. Volunteering is just putting yourself into life. If you have happiness in you, then you can volunteer.

The Great Spectrum of Volunteers

BRIAN O'CONNELL

The people you've already met in these pages and the others still to come provide some sense of the many different kinds of people who volunteer and the many ways they make a difference. As diverse and special as they are, however, even they can't convey the enormous variety of volunteers or the bewildering range of services they provide.

In almost fifty years of working with voluntary organizations, I've learned that most Americans and even most volunteer leaders don't know how widespread volunteering is in this country and therefore don't realize what a mighty force for good it is. So let me start with some numbers that I think you'll find quite surprising and wonderfully encouraging.

The first one I've said earlier, but I find that the enormity may not sink in the first time around so I'm going to repeat it here. One hundred million Americans volunteer. That's one out of every two of us over the age of thirteen.

On average, we give four hours a week to the causes of our choice.

Volunteers are poor and wealthy, young and old, men and women, employed and retired, conservative and liberal, urban and rural, people of all colors and races, and those who have problems themselves.

We are the only country in the world where volunteering is so pervasive a characteristic of the total society. Volunteering does exist everywhere but nowhere are the numbers, proportions, and spectrum of participation so great as here.

Our voluntary spirit is alive and growing. A far larger

proportion of our population is involved in community activity today than at any time in our history.

To the surprise of all who have assumed that with so many women now in the workplace it would be harder to find women volunteers, the happy reality is that there are more women than ever serving in these roles. Indeed, several surveys provide the fascinating information that the woman who works for pay is more likely to volunteer than the woman who does not. (The largest single reason people volunteer is that someone asks them, so the woman in the workplace is more likely to receive many requests.)

When one thinks of the giants among volunteers, one is likely to think of women such as Clara Barton, Jane Addams, Mary McLeod Bethune, Susan B. Anthony, Dorothea Dix, Alice Paul, Elizabeth Cady Stanton, Harriet Beecher Stowe, Dorothy Day, Elizabeth Seton, Carry Nation, Margaret Sanger, and Lucretia Mott. Volunteering, distinct from the private and public sectors, has routinely and traditionally tapped the full spectrum of the nation's talent.

For those who might have thought that volunteering is primarily a woman's activity, men represent about half of all volunteers and on average give just about the same number of hours.

For a while the so-called "baby boomers," those now 30 to 55 years old, were not nearly as involved as their parents had been. Once this late-marrying group began to have families, however, they wanted the same things their parents had—such as religious experiences, good communities, excellent schools, and stimulating cultural opportunities. They realized that to attain them required their participation. Now their levels of volunteering have caught up with everyone else's.

The even younger generation, the teens, have somehow caught the spirit and the habit very early. For those 14 to 18 years old, the involvement is remarkably high and growing. Sixty percent of them are volunteers, compared with the adult average of fifty percent. They give almost as much of their time, 3.5 hours a week compared to 4.2.

Today's volunteers are likely to be involved in advocacy efforts to deal with underlying causes of problems. For example, though they still want to help feed the hungry and house the homeless, they also want to prevent hunger and homelessness in the first place.

Volunteers are by far the greatest contributors of money to charitable causes. They give twice as much as those who are not volunteers, and their financial generosity is spread far beyond the organizations for which they volunteer.

The reason that this encouraging information probably surprises most readers is that volunteering is an aspect of our national life we have taken for granted and never felt a need to study. Now that there is a growing realization that volunteering is a vital part of our national makeup, there is greater interest in having a clearer grasp of the facts, trends, and impact. Not surprisingly, the more we learn, the more we rejoice. Increasingly, this society recognizes and celebrates the incredible number of people who are involved.

Volunteers usually work together to increase their reach and results. There are more than a million voluntary organizations in America today, ranging from small community groups to massive national crusades. They organize to serve every conceivable aspect of human need and aspiration and to influence almost every public issue.

The services of voluntary organizations extend from neighborhoods to the ozone layer and beyond. Whether one's interest is wildflowers or civil rights, arthritis or clean air, oriental art or literacy, the dying or the unborn, organizations are already at work, and if they don't suit our passion, it's still a special part of America that we can go out and start our own.

It is this joining together of compassion, spirit, and power that often makes the difference for the most serious issues facing all of us. Such enormous and complicated problems as cancer and poverty require thousands of volunteers focusing on service, prevention, public awareness, and public policy. Some of the best of volunteering in this country is accomplished by legions of people in humanitarian crusades.

When Richard Carter did his study of how voluntary health organizations and their volunteers had been able to make such a difference in areas as difficult as polio, heart disease, and tuberculosis, he realized that the country was seeing a new form of massive citizen participation focused on needs that couldn't be solved alone. He gave the book the wonderful title *The Gentle Legions.*

At times, to get attention and achieve results requires more than gentleness, but it still requires the legions. There are times when citizens have to get pretty agitated and vocal in order to call attention to needs and solutions. Senator Daniel Patrick Moynihan of New York says it is essential that free people have these "outlets for outrage."

No matter how one defines or describes the way Americans are involved, the central message is that millions of people serve in thousands of ways. Within all of their causes, volunteers perform a dizzying variety of activities. They inform, protest, assist, teach, heal, build, advocate, comfort, testify, support, solicit, canvas, demonstrate, guide, feed, criticize, organize, appeal, usher, contribute, and in hundreds of other ways, serve people and causes.

One hundred and fifty years ago, the French observer Alexis de Tocqueville characterized America's civic behavior as "habits of the heart." Fifty years ago the novelist F. Scott Fitzgerald expressed it: "America is a willingness of the heart." And now we celebrate one hundred million "voices from the heart."

Thanks to them, the nation's heart is stronger than ever.

KAREN VON DEN DEALE

BOOKKEEPER, AGE 50 **BREWSTER, MASSACHUSETTS**

Founder of Wild Care, a wildlife shelter and clinic

PHOTOGRAPHS BY PAUL FUSCO

When you volunteer, you have to pick your battles. My battle is wildlife preservation. I worked for years with children and I love them, but it was time to pick another battle.

I joke and say caring for animals is easier than raising kids because animals don't have to go to college and they never get pregnant before their time. But this is fulfilling a childhood dream. I grew up by Franklin Lake in New Jersey, and I was so mesmerized, so fascinated by the animal world there. I would spend all day there.

All I ever read about was animals. My room was always filled with tanks and jars of snakes and pollywogs and turtles. I wanted to be a veterinarian, and I had my mother take me to visit the director of the Bronx Zoo.

I had a sixth-grade teacher who taught me how to learn about animals. He was so in tune with what I felt and thought. He found a baby squirrel with a broken leg and gave it to me, but told me I had to write to Cornell University's veterinary school and find out how to take care of it. And I did.

"This kind of volunteering is a tough concept for some people," says Karen, founder of Wild Care, Inc., a nonprofit clinic for sick, injured, and orphaned animals. "They want to help the animals, but the less direct contact the wildlife has with people, the better." Here Karen prepares a turtle's warm bath so it won't hibernate, which slows healing.

I'm like most of the people I volunteer with: I've always had an insatiable desire to be with animals and to help animals. The more you become a part of the rehabilitation process, the more your reasons for being there evolve. It's wonderful when you grow from your volunteer work.

The focus of Wild Care is to get each animal healed and back out into nature. It's not like you're coming in and answering phones two hours a week. There's more responsibility involved: you're part of the healing process. You begin to see the personalities and tolerances of each animal, and you come to gain a respect for all creatures.

Baby birds have to be fed every fifteen to twenty minutes, from sun up to sun down. In July you're talking about a fourteen-hour day. We really have to be nurturers, but that's not always what the animals need. Most of the adult wildlife just need a safe, quiet place to heal themselves.

The first volunteers arrive at seven a.m. The turtles get a hot bath every morning; they need to have their body temperatures at a certain level or they won't eat. We go outside to clean the birds' cages. Then we go to the clinic and take care of the injured animals—birds with broken wings and small mammals that survived cat or dog attacks or were hit by a car or shot by people. We

stabilize and evaluate them, and if they need a veterinarian's care, there's one who lives a half mile away who volunteers for us.

Sometimes if I'm lucky I'll grab one quiet hour to myself during the day. Sometimes I have lunch; sometimes I don't. There's so much time needed to do the phones, write educational materials, and shop for the animals' food. I have to do a lot of fund-raising to pay the monstrous electric bill. It's a major part of my time. At night I do bookkeeping, and that's how I support myself.

Volunteers come in and out throughout the day, and bring in animals with them. I am incredibly grateful for them, for giving a piece of their lives to this work. Sometimes we get animals so far gone they cannot be rehabilitated. We're dedicated to each other, we sort of have a family here, but we do euthanize. That's when we have disputes.

This work has totally consumed my life. It's hard to explain. I've sacrificed some friendships for this. And I wish I could have started much sooner. I feel like I've wasted a lifetime. This is truly where I belong. I was always there, in my heart, but volunteering for the animals didn't happen until I caught up with the world. I wish I knew then what I know now. People won't care for wildlife until they make the connection that every little creature does its part to make this earth work.

When you commit to volunteering, there's also a time commitment. Most organizations are going to be flexible, but you have to decide what you want to do, be realistic about how much you can do, and commit that time to do it.

This work has given me an incredible respect for what goes on in our environment. This earth is alive. It's an evolving, living, changing thing. And all of us—whether we are red fire ants or the most beautiful eagle—are part of this living, breathing planet. Humankind is consuming everything, hurting whole species and contaminating the earth. I'm grateful now to have the gift of life. I'm grateful to help relieve pain and suffering to individual animals. I want to touch enough lives to help people realize that we have a responsibility. This kind of volunteering opens up your life, gives life a new dimension.

PREVIOUS PAGE: "Birds are clever, strong, and incredibly resourceful," says Karen, splinting a crow's foot. "The first time I cared for an injured bird, it was almost a religious experience."

Karen transfers a pigeon from the clinic to an outside recovery pen where it can recondition its flight muscles before release. Karen's wildlife refuge, set up in and around her home, has nursed everything from wild goslings to flying squirrels back to health before setting them free again.

PET TAXI

RUBEN REYES

MATH TEACHER, AGE 25 **PROVIDENCE, RHODE ISLAND**

Tutors kids in math and science

PHOTOGRAPHS BY LEONARD FREED

Learning is what volunteering, work, and life are all about for me.

When I started volunteering two years ago, I just wanted to do the right thing. Now it's more about the kids. I want them to know they can come to me for other problems. It's more like being a father figure than just a math tutor.

Teaching what's right and wrong, especially to kids who aren't learning that at home, is so important. I can tell when they're having problems that stem from growing up around violence.

Teaching kids to rely on each other and trust one another, that's a real legacy.

But their education comes first. I'm serious in class. I don't even smile until after Christmas break. I don't answer non-class questions until the last day of school. That works best. I learned that from my earlier teaching experiences. I let the kids know teaching is serious and their education is serious. What a teacher does takes time and preparation.

At Times[2], Inc., where I tutor, the kids are motivated. That's exciting for me. They're kids who want to pursue their education so it's easier to teach them. They learn to speak up and listen to each other, to respect one another and each other's opinions. It's a team effort, unlike some public school classrooms where one student might do all the work and others copy. Our program teaches kids to work things out among themselves. Kids learn better from each other. And I get to learn more about teaching and the kids.

When I work at the Perry Middle School, I have fifty minutes of class with the kids. When I volunteer, I have three hours with them. I get to learn their backgrounds, can share more, and can let them know I went through the same things they're going through now, having a single parent, dealing with violence in school.

If I hear a student say, "College is for smart people," I can tell them, "No, it's for people who want to learn." I got lucky: someone taught me to educate myself, and that's what I want to give back. I can't save everybody, but I can steer some, and because of my background, they understand where I'm coming from.

I'm Hispanic, and coming from the inner city, I can relate to the kids really well. I'm a young twenty-five, so it's easier for them to listen to me.

"When I started teaching, older teachers told me, 'These kids are monsters; they're going to tear you down,'"says Ruben, with student Leah Tosta. "I didn't listen to them."

"You don't know what kids are capable of," says Ruben. "Knowing they're learning from me keeps me coming back." Here David Alves and Teddy Awuah work to solve one of Ruben's algebra-based puzzles.

I'm not like grandpa lecturing them. During our free time at school, I'll go to the gym and play around so they can see me as a person and not just as a teacher. With the volunteer program, the kids can call me by my first name. It's more mature, we have adult interaction, and they don't give one-word answers, like at public school.

The Boys' Club of New York is significant in my life because it was there that I learned about a scholarship for a six-week summer program at a New England boarding school. I went to Maine with six other kids from the Club. I thrived in the smaller classrooms, and I told them I was interested in going to a boarding school in New England.

I wound up at St. Andrew boys' prep school in Rhode Island, and let me tell you, high school up here is such a safer environment than the city. I found out I was pretty good in math and later got a scholarship to Salve-Regina University in Newport. The dean there, who knew about my volunteer experience with youth in New York City, gave my name to Times[2]. I was honored to get involved. This is my second year.

From my senior year in high school to my senior year in college, I went back to the Boys' Club every summer. I had to give back to the Club what it gave me.

The only thing I really learned in New York City was how to watch my back in the streets. If a fight happened, I learned to leave the scene. I actually teach a little bit of that to my students now, how to avoid violence. It's just common sense. It worked for me.

I grew up with a single parent—just my mom and two younger brothers. My sixteen-year-old brother is following in my footsteps: he got the same scholarship, and is attending the same high school I did. Every time I'd go home for the holidays, I'd spend time with my brother and point out that there's nowhere to get a real education in the city. He felt the same way. I'm glad he and hopefully my younger brother will get a good education.

My background and my knowledge of math both come into play when I volunteer. It's equal. I provide general guidance, too. The headmaster of St. Andrew asked me if I know of any good students for scholarships, so I keep my eye out for students with that kind of potential. I'm really trying to do what people did to help me.

That's what I focus on every Saturday when I step into the classroom to volunteer my time. I want to let inner-city kids know that they don't have to give up on their education. I also want to teach them to be decent, well-rounded people.

I'm young and don't have any kids. I don't understand not volunteering if you're twenty-five and have no family to take care of. But to encourage someone to volunteer, they have to experience it. You can't tell people anything; they'll always have something else to do. So I take people with me if I want to encourage them. I trick them into it. If they volunteer for one day, it changes their perception, and they learn how hard and how rewarding it is.

ALISON OKINAKA

ATTORNEY, AGE 38 **SALT LAKE CITY, UTAH**

Uses her dogs to help physical therapy patients

PHOTOGRAPHS BY JOHN EISELE

I went to Smith College, then Harvard Law School, and worked for corporate law firms as soon as I graduated. For a few years I did volunteer legal work for people with AIDS. I got started at the last corporate law firm I worked for. This firm was serious about its pro bono program and had us work for people with AIDS who needed help with their wills, trusts, and powers of attorney. We often had to assess the patients' coherence before we could do anything, so we got to know them personally.

Most of these people really didn't have much, but we helped tie up loose ends and helped to put their minds at ease. You get to see how amazing people can be when you volunteer. They would be so sick, but so kind and so polite and appreciative. It was surprising, when you think of the extreme circumstances they were in. People rise to the occasion.

In a big law firm, you're pretty much a drone, following orders. But volunteering once or twice a week—this was dealing with people. It took more responsibility.

I have selfish reasons for volunteering, although other people benefit. I know people who volunteer so many hours every day. I don't put in that kind of time, so it's hard for me to think of myself as a volunteer. The legal volunteering was more service-oriented and structured. That structure helped me deal with seeing someone in such a sad state of health. I tried to control my emotions; no one wants a volunteer to come in and start weeping. Now, I work with a rehabilitation hospital. People there are learning how to walk again after hip

Alison and Roxy, one of her dogs, cheer up Helen Cazier before her physical therapy session. Alison volunteers with InterMountain Therapy, a nonprofit organization specializing in animal-assisted therapy.

ALISON

"The dogs help to motivate people in physical therapy," says Alison, who undertook specialized training to work with licensed therapists and handle pets in medical care settings. "My role is really secondary." Here her corgi Brewster gets ready to chase a ball thrown by Stephen Park, paralyzed after a car accident.

replacement surgery or car accidents. There's more interaction and less structure. It's more personal and involves me as much as the patient. This was hard when I first started out.

I bought two corgi dogs when I moved to Utah in 1992. "Corgi" is Welsh for "dwarf dog." Roxy looks like a stuffed teddy bear, and Brewster looks like a little fox.

InnerMountain Therapy has the outlook that animals really do a lot for the people, more than just comfort them. It seems they recover faster. You know when you're out walking your dog, and people come up and approach you and talk to you? The dogs help. I don't know if I could walk into a room of strangers who are sick and try to interact. The patients just rush over and start hugging the dogs. The next thing you know they're your best friends.

I like volunteering with my dogs because I never really liked being in the spotlight myself very much. Having them as the focus of attention is more my temperament. I'm getting less shy doing this. It forces me to get out and meet strangers every week.

I have mixed feelings sometimes when I volunteer. Results are what I'm looking for. Like people who are in a coma who seem to respond to the dogs when they cuddle up to them or lick their faces. But you don't always see the positive results. It happens, but not always when you're around. This makes you think, "What if I did more?"

Volunteering always does more than people think it does. I do it because it makes me appreciate how fortunate I am. I get upset with my husband when he doesn't empty the dishwasher. Then I see stroke patients and children who have been abused. It's selfish, but I realize how lucky I am. Most people think about how oppressed they are. It's kind of like therapy for me.

To be honest, most weeks I don't feel like going. It's near the end of the week, I'm tired, and I tell myself, "I'm not going to do this anymore." But I'm always glad I've done it after I'm done. These little things make a big difference in people's lives and it means a lot to me. I feel like I'm a lucky person. I realize it through this work. I don't have kids, and this allows me to be around them.

Volunteering allows you to fulfill certain needs you have in your life. It helps you grow. I used to have a fear of hospitals and people who are ill. Volunteering helped me deal with it when my mother and mother-in-law were both sick and later died.

I used to think people would forget us once we are gone, but they don't. People remember your presence. That means a lot.

BEN SMILOWITZ

HIGH SCHOOL STUDENT, AGE 16 **WEST HARTFORD, CONNECTICUT**

Cofounder of the International Student Activism Alliance

PHOTOGRAPHS BY DIRCK HALSTEAD

Volunteering, to me, isn't only washing windows or working at nursing homes—not that these things aren't important. It's also making things better by speaking up for what you believe in and getting people organized.

At last summer's Presidential Summit, five presidents and General Colin Powell came together, but not a lot of students were there. If you're going to talk about carrying the volunteer spirit into the next century, you need to have young people involved. It's my hope that the nation's leaders and the people behind the recent push for volunteerism recognize this side of volunteering.

The ISAA is about a year and half old, and we already have 145 chapters nationwide. I think this is proof that teenagers are taking on the stereotype that all students are apathetic—and proving otherwise. Our mission is to promote student activism, network among ourselves, and empower each other. We want to have a say in decisions that affect our lives.

Students involved with ISAA will all go on to vote when they turn eighteen, because they see how important it is to let your opinions be heard. They'll stay involved. A lot of students ask me before joining, "What have you done in the past? Why will anyone listen to you?" I tell them if you yell loud enough, people will hear you. If you go to the media the right way, it gives them no choice but to address the issue. Everyone in ISAA learns how to write a press release. We got a response from our state governor the same day we put a press release online.

The Vermont chapter of ISAA is trying to ban child labor abuses and put a student on the state board of education. A Florida chapter is speaking

"We want to make sure students are being heard because we have a lot to share," says Ben, talking with student leaders assembled for a national conference called Planning for a National Youth Movement.

out on a new dress code. Another chapter is fighting for gender equality on sports teams.

This is advocacy. The students involved are volunteers, speaking up on behalf of other students. We're helping ourselves have a strong voice in decisions that affect us, and I think we're starting to have an impact. We want people to know what we feel is important. We want to make changes.

Chairing the ISAA, I average at least thirty-five hours a week volunteering. Some weeks more. I can't let it slide. I usually procrastinate with my school work, but this is stuff I really want to do.

Finding the energy? I sleep in on weekends. As long as I can keep my grades up, I'll devote all my spare time to the ISAA. I'm always inspired by working with other students. Every student I talk to gives me an extra hour of energy.

Someone called me from Houston yesterday, wanting to get involved. I make keeping in touch with people a priority because you can lose that when you do the "busy work" for an organization. Delegating is a high priority for us; our state coordinators give everyone something to do. The West Virginia chapter has become self sufficient; they write their own press releases. In Vermont, they're so efficient they got a grant to pay for their phone, travel, mailing, and E-mail accounts. I like seeing that happen. Starting this group, I realize how much money it takes to do anything. But you can't let finances deter you. There's always a way.

Connecticut and other school systems around the country have "zero-tolerance" rules. If you're caught with a knife or any kind of drug, you're tossed out immediately. Hey! Whoa! We live in America! There's something called "due process" and rights that even kids in school are entitled

to. This is serious stuff, but students want to look into each situation; one size doesn't fit all.

I had the idea for ISAA after I met Mark Talisman, a political advisor on Israeli issues, at a conference in D.C. when I was fourteen. He was talking about atrocities in Africa and church fires in African-American churches. He asked me, "What if these were synagogues? You'd be all over it." When I got back to Connecticut, I started making calls to community groups and churches, and put together a candlelight vigil for the African-American churches that had been burned down in just eight days. We got together three hundred people and raised $8,000. Our congressman and different religious leaders came on short notice to speak. I was amazed when I realized that the same thing could be done for student issues.

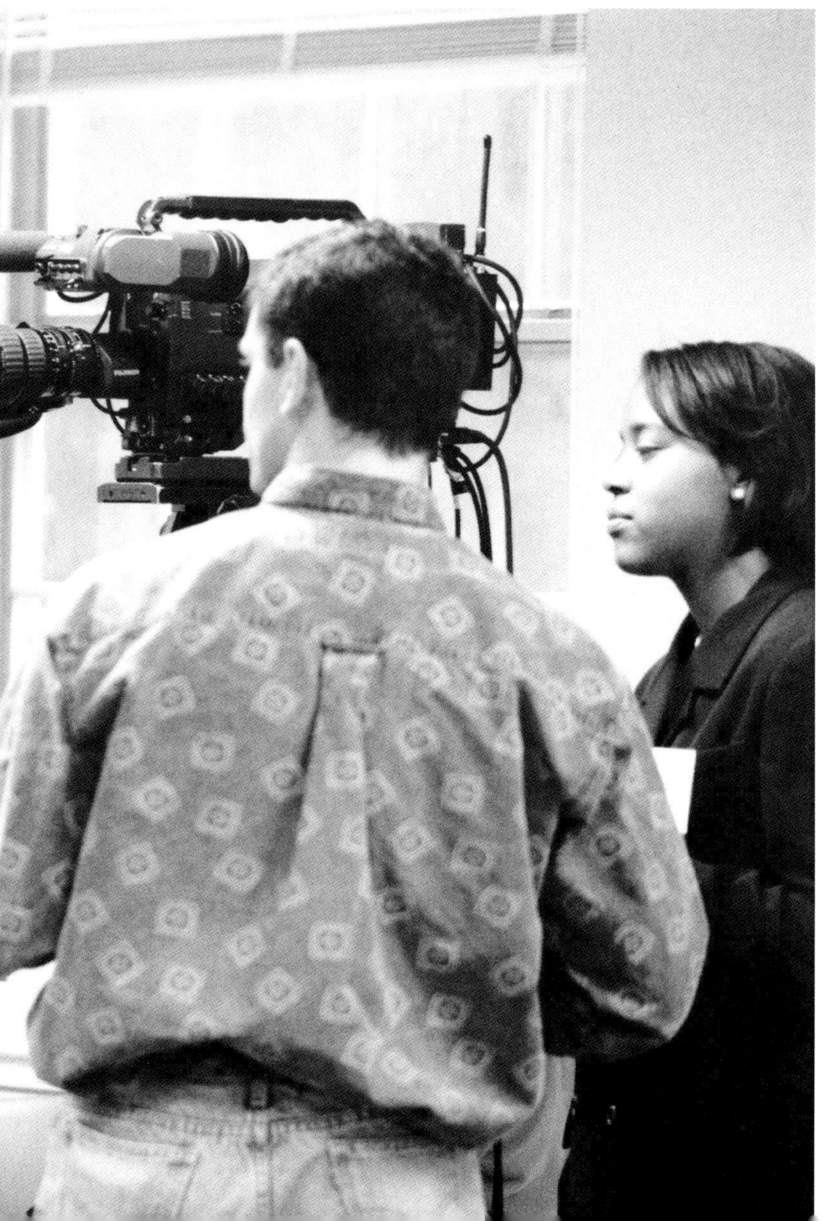

Of course, my parents help out. They drive me to airports at odd hours of the night. They drive me to fax machines. They let me go to all these conferences. And when I get really upset about something, they help calm me down. That's hard to do sometimes because I care so much about these issues.

Anyone who thinks young people don't care or don't want to get involved should check out the new volunteers for the ISAA. These are fifteen-year-olds who never even used to vote on student issues. Now look at them. They're on radio programs. They're talking with Congress. They're on TV.

"You get on TV and direct something to an elected official," says Ben, here being interviewed about student activism, "and you get a response. It really works."

SEAN O'BYRNE

SCREENWRITER, AGE 40 **CULVER CITY, CALIFORNIA**

Teaches yoga and meditation to prison inmates

PHOTOGRAPHS BY JOE BUISSINK

I teach chi gong, a form of exercise that blends hatha yoga and meditation. The concept of yoga before meditation is to prepare the inmates mentally, emotionally, and physically for an internal experience. Inmates who are committed to the practice don't get into trouble; they don't get "points" against them on their records. Many are actually moved to lesser-security prisons.

The Prison Project is taught everywhere, at Chino, San Quentin, Riker's Island, and in prisons in Mexico, Venezuela, France, Canada, and Australia. For the last three years, I've been teaching at FCI-Terminal Island in San Pedro, a federal prison. A few men are in their early fifties, but a lot of prisoners are young men, twenty-five to thirty-five. It's a mixed group of white, black, and Hispanic men. About fifty men take the *Satsang*—a term for keeping the company of others who are seeking the truth on a spiritual path.

The most profound change is that the men have opened up to each other. When they started the *Satsang,* they had no eye contact with each other, no sharing with other inmates. There was no sense of deep friendship between the inmates; what they had was more like an alliance of security. After three years, there's a whole new life in each man. There's a sense of optimism, joy, even a sense of freedom. They have a new respect and connection with each other. They're close friends now, and have become their own community within the prison. This mutual support is needed to pursue a life in prison.

I know people in prison who have no opportunity to pursue worldly dreams. They're shut out from their families, from loved ones, from careers, from all the things we take for granted and pursue. But in spite of this, they have found a deep and profound peace and a self-awareness that allows them to live with respect, even though they're coming to terms with the illegal things they did and making amends to the people they harmed. I believe that when these men get out of prison, if given an opportunity, they will never go back.

I'm grateful to witness these men finding that peace. And I'm grateful for the volunteers who have helped. I used to feel volunteering was "doing the right thing." Now I'm honored to be among these men who have become giving, respectful people in this environment. The lights are on in their eyes. They welcome us into their community, and it's a wonderful thing to be part of.

"I went into these prisons as a teacher," says Sean, here playing the harmonium. "I was taking in tools they didn't have. What we've graduated to is a mutual, respectful friendship." Sean's class is part of the Prison Project, a program founded by Siddha Meditation Center of Los Angeles, a nondenominational spiritual institute.

"The men in prison, especially those facing twenty-five years to life, are faced with the brutal reality that they're confined," says Sean. "Yoga is a way for them to find internal freedom." Here the men practice a Warrior pose, a posture that embodies the qualities of nobility, courage, and compassion.

I was invited to an awards banquet at FCI three years ago, put on by prisoners for the volunteer organizations. Everyone was there—AA, NA, Catholic Social Services—four hundred volunteers in all. We were served dinner by the prisoners; they cooked, they cleared the plates, they were dressed in their finest, cleaned, pressed prison outfits. They sang choir songs and read poetry and passages from the Bible. I could feel they were showing their gratitude. I saw the fruition of volunteer work. And the Prison Project was picked as an outstanding program. It was an incredibly special night in my life.

What's so powerful is that this work means freedom for me as well. In my life, I begin to feel imprisoned. The week before I go in, I'll think, "I'm far too busy to do this." But every single time I've come out of that prison, I feel grateful for the time I was there. Five years ago, I came in thinking I was going to save them, but what I've found is that volunteering has helped me save myself. It transcends job titles and bank accounts. It's about freedom that's in the heart.

That's the great thing about meditation with the prisoners. It's not teaching them to be sappy and weak. It means these guys are finding new levels of respect for themselves and all things.

Our mission is for everyone to find a personal freedom, no matter where they are. Freedom on the inside. Inmates learn to feel freedom inside prison walls and freedom from fear and doubts that each one of us feels.

The program teaches the spirit of volunteerism by teaching the idea of selfless service. The only way we can teach this is to do it ourselves. Whenever anything is given in a sense of volunteerism, it enhances one's vision to see what is beneficial and what is pleasurable, the long-term versus short-term. The prisoners involved with the program have the mental and emotional space to discriminate between the two. More and more, they are choosing what is beneficial to their lives over immediate pleasures. They're going to school, learning trades, running; they're in the top 5 percent in everything. They've reestablished contact with their families. They've found a life again.

I'm not an apologist for people who commit crimes. But I believe that imprisonment alone doesn't change anything. There needs to be some rehabilitation, and that usually falls on volunteers, people who are willing to go in there and be friends with prisoners, to offer hope and a kind of compassionate friendship men don't find in prison. These guys are touched that people care and will reach out and make an effort to be with them. That's what a real friend does. And there are intangible rewards that come back from that. People are attracted to volunteering because they want to do good, and that leads to the secret bounty of giving—you get back way more than you give.

The spirit of volunteerism has been around a long time. My father's generation fought in a world war and really sacrificed. That spirit of giving ebbs and flows. We're coming to a time when we realize that the overall health of the community reflects on each individual's health, so we have to look out for everyone, even those people on the streets.

Every time after class, the prisoners grab my hand and look me in the eye, to let me know they mean it when they say "thank you."

"As a community, if we can offer opportunities for rehabilitation, it will make for a better community when the men are released," says Sean. Here they practice "floating palms," a tai chi pose.

TOMMY CHESBRO

COMMUNITY HEALTH EDUCATOR, AGE 37 **TULSA, OKLAHOMA**

HIV prevention speaker, educator, and organizer

PHOTOGRAPHS BY ALEX WEBB

I've been HIV positive since 1985. I keep some signs in my office with messages that help inspire me on days when I'm tired or frustrated. My favorite one says, "If there's a barrier preventing you from your path, go where there is no path and leave a trail." That's my philosophy of life. I don't think anything will ever change if you don't forge your own path at some point in your life.

When I do workshops for pregnant teens, I try to get them to learn something from my past and stay away from the situation I'm in.

They want to hear about sexual behavior and relationships even though they're hearing this from a gay man. They identify with what I have to say about what's a healthy relationship and what isn't. They relate to issues of self esteem. I was a young person; I partied but I had dreams. Where I am now is not what I dreamt about. There are consequences for everything we do in our lives, and whether it's positive or negative sometimes depends on how we react, not just on the action that led to a situation.

Coming from two different cultures—Cherokee and Caucasian—opens a lot of doors for me. I've been able to speak with Indian communities where I wouldn't be allowed if I wasn't a mixed-blood person. Going into Indian communities or schools, having something in common with the people I'm talking to, makes it easier to get the message across.

Teaching about sexuality in Oklahoma public schools has some challenges. They will limit you on this subject. Smaller school systems won't allow an educator to talk about needle cleaning; it's seen as promoting drug use. I have a reputation for being very open, so I'm not invited to

"Being HIV positive adds meaning to the work I do," says Tommy, after his AIDS prevention workshop for pregnant teenagers. "Those of us who have this disease bring our perspective to educating the public."

many public schools. I don't go to schools where I can't talk about condoms or answer every question honestly.

When I volunteer to promote HIV testing, everything I say depends on who's in my audience and how much time I have. If it's a limited time with a large group of people, then I just want to get as many people as possible to take the test after my talk. If I'm in front of a mixed audience, kids and adults, I may not get too personal. But if I'm asked a tough question, I'll answer it honestly.

Volunteering for nonprofits in the field of AIDS—planning, organizing, and chairing different organizations—is completely different from the direct education volunteering I do, but the goal is the same: Take care of those who are infected and prevent others from getting the disease.

A lot of my volunteer work overlaps with my paid work, too, so I have to find a balance between that and my personal life. I have to find time for myself—like I went hunting all this weekend with my father. You can become completely overwhelmed with your volunteer work. I have to decide when I'm willing or not willing to do a project, just to keep my sanity. I'm so committed to the cause, though, I can't imagine myself not doing what I do as a volunteer.

Twelve years ago I never thought this is what I would be doing with my life. I was in musical theater and loved to perform and sing. I was getting a master's degree in performing arts, but I dropped out when I found out I was HIV positive. I was so devastated, and there weren't a lot of people to turn to for support.

I got into public health out of a need to do something about my HIV infection. I had to learn

"I have to be totally honest and forthcoming," says Tommy. "Kids find out really quickly if you're fake, so I talk openly about my past, where I came from, and what got me to my situation now."

about the disease. I had to learn how to live with it and deal with my life. I met someone who spoke publicly about his HIV status and AIDS awareness. I was moved and inspired by his courage and commitment. I took classes with the Health Department in counseling and HIV testing and education, and when that young man died in February 1991, they asked me to do his job. I accepted. It was a way for me to fight back.

You can't fully understand the consequences of the disease—physically, emotionally, socially, economically—unless you have it. Being HIV positive, you have to learn to face your fears fully or let them destroy you.

Across the board, there's still prejudice and stigma associated with AIDS because of how it's spread. Drug use and sexuality are topics people don't want to hear about or talk about. They don't think AIDS is something that can happen to people in Oklahoma. They're more aware, now that it's in our community, but too many people still don't believe it will ever happen to them. They don't think they're at any kind of risk.

So you could say I have my work cut out for me. Every morning, I have so much to do. On a heavy week, I'll devote about forty hours to volunteer work. I'm lucky that my employer, the Indian Health Care Resource Center, will allow me to do some of these things on work time. On an average week, I'll volunteer for ten to fifteen hours, easily.

HIV and AIDS educators who have died from the disease give me tremendous inspiration, give me the energy to do what I do every day. Those people had the courage to face who they were and try to change things, and I want to continue that. Someone has to keep telling the story—otherwise people will forget.

Probably the best reward for me is when somebody comes up to me who is living with HIV, but has never talked to another person about it. It's been bottled up inside, and I'm the first person trusted to hear about it. Helping just one person makes a difference.

It sounds cliché, but while one match will barely light a room, a hundred will light up the whole room. Every little bit contributes to the whole. There's more work to be done than any one person can do, so anything a person can do for his or her community will make it stronger.

I've learned a lot in the last few years about being a whole person. You can't just take. You have to give back. It's part of the balance of life.

PATRICIA WRIGHT

CHOIR DIRECTOR, AGE 54 **SEATTLE, WASHINGTON**

Founded and directs the Total Experience Gospel Choir

PHOTOGRAPHS BY ED KASHI

If you expect to get paid for everything, life can be very boring. To volunteer means there are no strings attached, because you do what you want to do and you do it with more passion and excitement. Everyone needs a vocation that pays them, but there's a sense of spontaneity and freedom with volunteering. I never know what I'm going to sing for many events until I get there and feel the spirit of the place and the people I am singing for. Most of the young people in the choir have been with me for ten years, so they're ready for anything. They trust me.

I volunteered for United Way for years, for the prison ministries and the emergency food program, and I do fund-raising for everybody. You need to give back to the same universe that gave you life. I sing at children's hospitals. Retirement homes and nursing homes, I sing for them. We can walk into the saddest situation, say the children's hospital, and just to see the look on the children's faces is like receiving a million bucks that you didn't know was coming.

I'm a preacher's kid, so I started doing music at the age of three. That's when I did my first solo. Then, between 1970 and 1976, the school system had a gospel music experiment program. I was doing a gospel show Sunday mornings at a black radio station and was the choir director of my church. I was asked to teach in the school program. My first class had one black student, five Asians, and twenty whites.

I taught at five different schools. The administration thought it was the coolest thing. We went to a national jazz festival in Reno, Nevada, and took second place. Black students started getting involved then. Later it became equally black, Asian, and white.

"Almost thirty years ago, I had a vision in my sleep of directing a young choir that would entertain and help people around the world," says Pat, who has taught more than five hundred gospel students over the years. "Now I call them my children and grandchildren."

Total Experience was born once I got wind that the program was going to end. I thought I'd turn it into a community choir, not part of the church or the school. The first meeting, 108 people showed up, from four years old to eighteen. That was September of 1973.

We had no name at the time. But we combined with other high school gospel choirs, and one called themselves the Black Experience Choir. I called the unified choir the Total Experience because it involved all people.

We started our volunteer efforts in 1980. The church we were with felt our choir was taking all the members and musicians from the church choir, and we were asked to leave. But getting kicked out was the best thing that happened to us. We became incorporated as a nonprofit and were truly independent. We began to branch out

"When I started the Gospel Choir, there was some resentment from people who felt it wasn't traditional enough," says Pat, with her twelve-member choir singing in Seattle's Key Arena at halftime between the SuperSonics and the Boston Celtics. "We let anyone interested in vocal music—black, Asian, white—join the group."

from competitions and move on to support social work.

We've been all over the U.S. and in twelve countries. In 1986 we flew to Nicaragua. We raised the money to go, almost $30,000. They had nothing there. It had all been bombed, and most of the parents had been killed. The area was run by seventeen- and eighteen-year-olds. They took us to the orphanages, and we sang there and at the hospitals. I cried most of the tour. So much death and pain. They didn't speak English but they got the message.

I think a lot of people, when they hear what we do, are inspired to volunteer in different ways.

"I'm not afraid to sing across the lines," says Pat. "We were the first African-American choir to visit the Mormon headquarters in Salt Lake City. I don't care what church you belong to. We'll sing anywhere where the door opens."

They wonder how we travel, how I spend so much time with the kids. I just do it. My advice is just do it and do it for free. There will be a time when you'll be paid in some way. Do it with no strings attached. Do it because you love it. Over five hundred kids have gone through the choir in the last twenty-four years. They're like my kids, and you don't get tired of your kids.

I don't remember anywhere in the Bible where Jesus was paid for what he did. He gave freely of himself, like the disciples and apostles after him. Somebody does the planting, somebody does the watering, somebody does the fertilizing, and then somebody else has to carry on. My job is to till the soil so that someone else can do the planting.

We're called the "bridge builders" in Seattle. We sing in Asian situations, black situations, gay situations, straight situations. We sing across denominational lines. I don't care what church you belong to. We'll sing anywhere where the door opens.

Despite all of the obstacles thrown in your way, if you know this is a direction you want your life to go in, let no one stop you. Volunteering has taught me this. What are you waiting for?

Building the Service Commitment of Today's Young People and All Future Generations

BRIAN O'CONNELL

Because America's level of volunteering is so important to the kind of people and nation we are, it's essential to understand and nurture the roots that give rise to such participation.

It's particularly important to build the service commitment and habit of young people. We cannot take for granted that it will happen. Many who have studied the generosity of Americans have warned and predicted that some day we would lose it. Even in his admiring portrait of us more than a hundred years ago, de Tocqueville feared we could not sustain our "habits of the heart."

What can we do—what must we do—to keep it alive? One of Alexis de Tocqueville's followers, Harriet Martineau, may have provided a clue when she said we must be sure that our "charity has gone deep as well as spread wide."

Research is beginning to tell us what enabled us to carry the traditions forward over the past 250 years and to give us clues of what we can do to "grow it deep and wide" into future generations.

It's becoming clear that there are six primary factors that determine if a young person is likely to become an active volunteer as an adult. Those factors are summarized in a recent book from INDEPENDENT SECTOR called *Care and Community in Modern Society: Passing on the Traditions of Service to Future Generations.* Essentially, young people grow up to be active volunteers if they:

1. Had parents or other adult role models who volunteered.
2. Were involved themselves in a youth group or other voluntary organization.
3. Were involved in a religious congregation where they were volunteers or were introduced to volunteer assignments outside the congregation.

4. Were exposed to volunteering as part of school activity.

5. Saw respected young peers volunteer.

6. Were influenced by favorable media coverage of volunteering.

If all or most of these factors are present, a young person is almost certain to become an active community figure. For example, if both parents volunteered, there is a 75 percent likelihood that their children will become volunteers. Sixty percent will be volunteers if only one parent volunteered. Among children whose parents did not volunteer, fewer than 40 percent will volunteer as adults.

Scott Rosenberg reflects this family model:

My parents were both active in the civil rights movement and were part of the peace movement during the 1960s. My father is a social worker and my mother is a lawyer specializing in domestic violence. So I guess it's not a stretch to say I grew up with a sense of social justice.

Fortunately, several of the key influences are getting even stronger. Many more schools are introducing students to volunteering and are adding classroom learning about what such service means to our society. That activity is burgeoning from kindergarten through high school and into colleges. Dr. Virginia A. Hodgkinson, principal author of the INDEPENDENT SECTOR study, reports that "schools that encourage voluntary service triple the participation rate of volunteering among young people."

Teenager Ben Smilowitz says:

Students are being heard because we have a lot to share [and] students involved will all go on to vote when they turn 18, because they see how important it is to let your opinions be heard. They'll stay involved.

Associations serving youth are also doing a great deal to encourage volunteering. For example, the Boy Scouts and Girl Scouts now have merit badges for volunteering and 4-H currently has ads running nationwide through the Ad Council with the theme Are You Into It? aimed at encouraging more youth to volunteer in their communities. Also, there are new and increasingly influential organizations dedicated primarily to youth service and they are playing an important role in enlarging the pool of younger volunteers. Such groups include the National Youth Leadership Council, Youth Service America, AmeriCorps, and Campus

Compact, which involves more than 700 college and university presidents who have united in commitment to community service for their institutions and students.

By spreading and strengthening the involvement of schools, congregations, youth serving organizations and others, we are likely to see the rewards for many years to come. A wonderful side benefit is what young volunteers think about the experience. Again, according to Dr. Hodgkinson:

"When teens were asked what benefits they derived from their volunteer service, the results were somewhat surprising, because some scholars assumed that the primary benefits would be self-serving, such as learning new skills or getting one's foot in the door for a future job. In fact, teens reported that the primary benefits they derived from their volunteering were learning to respect others, gaining satisfaction from helping others, learning to be helpful and kind, and learning to get along with and relate to others. Finally, in order of frequency, they reported that the benefits they derived from volunteering were that they learned new skills and that they learned to understand people who were different from themselves. If we were to provide a list of learning outcomes to be derived from volunteering, we could not come up with a better list."

New studies are also beginning to show that student volunteers get better grades, have fewer disciplinary problems, and stay in school. Those are wonderfully special extra benefits.

By understanding and working at the six primary factors that get young people started and keep them involved lifelong, we have our best chance to pass along the caring tradition to future generations. We need to be certain that all the key players—parents, religious organizations, schools, voluntary organizations, peers, and media—understand their responsibility and are resolved to fulfill it.

The very future of America as we know it is at stake.

RICHARD SPAIN

CATTLE FARMER, AGE 53 **LIMESTONE, TENNESSEE**

Leads cattle farming workshops for Appalachian farmers

PHOTOGRAPHS BY ED KASHI

Farming is in my family. My father and grandfather were farmers who raised cattle, grew cotton—whatever it took to make a living. I'm the youngest of nine kids and grew up around dairy cows and beef cattle.

Though I moved around a bit in the past, I always wanted to get back to farming. I missed the life. I missed the animals, working outside by myself, watching things grow. It's as much a lifestyle as it is a job. I love it, but you have to make a living doing it.

I started volunteering last year for Rural Resources. I met a fellow who was looking for participants for the Master Livestock Volunteer School, a class covering every aspect of beef cattle farming, from management to raising livestock. It was free, but you had to agree to donate forty hours of your time back to the farming community. So I started volunteering with the kids' show at the county fair. Show cattle is big business out here, and kids learn early how to groom cattle and take care of them. They're farm kids who compete against each other for ribbons, just to keep them interested in the farms. This school had one real aim: farmland preservation.

When I got more involved, they wanted me to start a "beef roundtable" to teach other farmers better cattle raising and management techniques. I was the only farmer in my area to make any kind of profit last year, and the bottom line about farming is it's got to be profitable.

These days there's something called "holistic resource management" of farms, which just means you maintain your farm as a whole; everything you do has to be good for you, your livestock, and the land. We're correcting over a

hundred years of mismanagement on these farms, which has led to water pollution and land erosion. People need to know that everything—the environment, the animals, and the humans—has its place. If you do what's good for everything, you're going to thrive. Fescue grass, for instance, isn't the best grass out there, but it's good for holding hills together and puts organic

"There's a real satisfaction that comes from helping people," says Richard. "If you can change someone's outlook for the better, it's worth your time."

matter back in the soil, so farmers can produce more bushels of corn without chemical fertilizer.

This is grass country. The right grass can help our cattle and build our soil. This is what our workshops are all about. The worst thing farmers do out here is allow continuous grazing and over-grazing. They'll have a twenty-acre pasture and twice the number of cattle that should be on it. They graze it into the ground, the soil doesn't recover, and that's where erosion starts.

We have to think about grazing management because it's a global market. Can U.S. farmers compete? A guy in Ireland doubles his net worth every four years using a rental farm. New Zealand is even more advanced than Ireland. We produce one hundred pounds of milk for $100. In Ireland they do it for $6. In New Zealand they do it for $4.

In Tennessee, we don't own the cows we raise; we buy calves from other herds in Oklahoma, Kansas, and Texas. We have the best grass in America. We also have the biggest concentration of beef cattle—and bigger herd sizes than they have in Texas. There's more beef cattle per square mile in this area than anywhere in the U.S.

What I helped do was gather producers, bankers, economists from the University of Tennessee;

"People want to learn a better way of farming, and I'm willing to share my knowledge," says Richard. "Farming is more than making a profit. It's part of the culture here."

and we all discussed the prospect of finishing beef here and selling locally grown beef. I put together a stocker co-op, a strictly nonprofit effort run entirely by volunteers. I get people to commit calves, make sure they meet weight and size guidelines, and help get them ready for market.

And we've found a better way to market them. All of our cattle are sold by video. A guy comes out to videotape cattle in the pasture and catalog the load number, the different kinds of cows, the weight and size of the cattle. The first Tuesday of every month the video is sent to potential buyers around the country. They make conference calls and make bids to auctioneers by phone, taking the place of the fair. This is much easier on cattle because they don't have to be transported around. We have a saying: "The average cow has seen more of the U.S. than the farmer who raised it." We're trying to teach people more humane ways to run their farms.

I feel if I volunteer my time, we can get more folks involved and then get more brain trusts out here to help. The local Cattlemen's Association is going to get involved soon. Last workshop, we had economists and agronomists out to the farm. We're showing people that humane farming can be done. People are hungry for knowledge. They stay outside for these workshops when it's so doggone cold they can't breathe and they're turning blue.

"Richard's working relationships with the beef farmers is what got these workshops off the ground," says Karen Childress, here with Richard and her husband, Larry. Karen and Larry are cofounders of Rural Resources, the nonprofit farming organization where Richard volunteers.

This volunteer work has given me hope. People are thinking. That's the best way you change people, through education. But it's hard to change farmers. They say, "That's how daddy did it and granddaddy did it."

The more we can do for environmental conservation, the less we'll be forced to do in the future. I don't mind putting in the work now. And I see that people with Rural Resources are more dedicated than any other group or any farmer in this area. They're getting involved with young people, and getting them out into the farm community with hands-on experience.

I don't know what happened to this country. People quit helping people. Everybody's too busy. We've become so caught up in ourselves. I'm as busy as the next guy, but it doesn't hurt to pull a half-day here and there to help somebody.

EMILY IRISH

WAITRESS AND BOOKSTORE CLERK, AGE 20 **WASHINGTON, D.C.**

Teaches self-defense and counsels young women on sexual assault

PHOTOGRAPHS BY CHIEN-CHI CHANG

I decided to check out the Empower Program, a nonprofit martial arts school that teaches rape prevention, during my sophomore year in high school. My older sister had suggested I try martial arts or kickboxing as a form of exercise. Back then, I wasn't into working out or concerned about being attacked as a woman. At fifteen, I was kind of at the bottom of the social ladder at school, and I was looking for a place to belong.

There was a "feeding order" at my school, and the older girls could be brutal to the younger ones—spreading rumors, ruining reputations, making fun of their clothes, just ostracizing them. There were upper-class students from my school who were taking the martial arts classes I enrolled in, and I got to know them. That was the first impact the program had on my life. The older students got to know me and would say "hi" to me in the halls between classes. This recognition changed the social order for me in school.

I found a group of friends I felt safe around, a group of people who like me and trust me and see my potential. That's what I would say to anyone thinking about volunteering. You may not only find your mission in life, but you will most likely find community, too. The people you work with and the people you help become your new family.

"If a woman is assertive, the attacker will often back off," says Emily, teaching a group of women at the Empower Program how to throw an elbow strike.

When I was sixteen, I started volunteering for the program as an office worker. I did basic filing and kept track of class lists and programs. That summer, the cofounder of the project, Rosalind Wiseman, was working on a book, *Defending Ourselves: A Guide to Prevention, Self-Defense, and Recovery from Rape,* which had a directory of sexual assault and rape crisis centers around the nation. I did the research for that directory and learned a lot about rape, sexual assault and the way women are socialized. I learned a lot about myself, too.

I had gotten into a relationship that was emotionally abusive when I was sixteen. It wasn't physical abuse; it was more subtle, verbal abuse. I caught a lot of degrading comments and coldness. It lasted two years. Although this relationship occurred when I began teaching classes and counseling other women with similar problems, I had a difficult time getting out of that situation. I don't know if I could have left that relationship without what I had learned from the Empower Program.

When I teach a class, I keep in mind the emotional states and the esteem levels of the women who take the self-defense courses. It wasn't until I experienced my own power as a fighter that I even felt comfortable being independent. I was told my whole life that I was weak, that I need a man to protect me and take care of me. After one year I gained the confidence to live my life. That's why I want to keep doing it.

Over the years, my skills have reached a point where I can teach any self-defense class—from the basic techniques course, where we learn to counter the common attack scenarios like being grabbed from behind; to the verbal techniques, where we learn how to stop a fight without engaging physically. This is the toughest class for many women, even those who are world-class athletes. Women grow up

speaking in a whisper, being quiet, deferring to others. In the verbal-technique class, we learn to yell and scream "No!" at the top of our lungs.

Something like 82 percent of all attackers are "ambivalent." They're looking for an easy victim to feed their egos. They're not really committed to hurting someone.

Teaching the classes is tough, demanding work physically. We work with the fundamentals of martial arts—kicks, strikes, balance, and breathing—but we keep it practical and effective for the street fight. The classes take about six hours a week, and I also spend time preparing, meeting students, and driving them home. It probably adds up to ten hours a week. We also coordinate Youth and Violence workshops for boys and girls at schools, teach classes in substance abuse at shelters for women and children, and hold demonstrations at shopping malls and in workplaces.

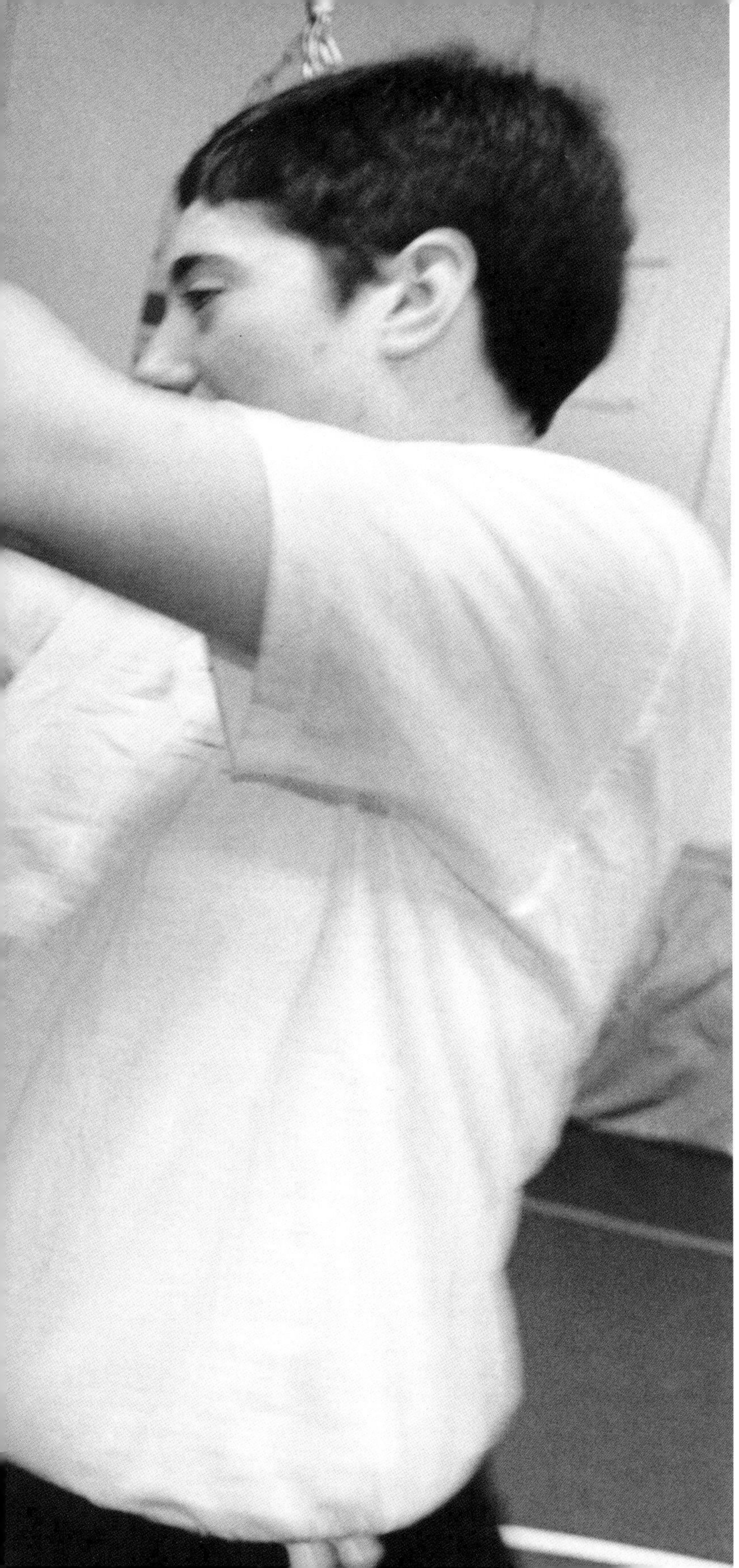

It isn't easy. I'm a waitress and hostess, I work part-time in a women's bookstore, and sometimes I tutor Spanish for extra money. It's hard making ends meet in D.C.

The classes can also be intense emotionally. I was teaching a course on sexual assaults and pins, where women are taught how to fight on the ground and use their lower-body strength to get attackers off of them, and three students were in tears throughout the entire class. Any kind of sexual assault scenario is going to bring up horrible memories and emotions for some women. One of the students was raped in her home and the whole, awful ordeal lasted six hours. Before it was her turn to fight, I told her, "You don't have to be alone this time." Emotional support is a fundamental part of the class.

The best thing we do is promote emotional healing. Emotional abuse has the most impact in our society and is the most common form of abuse. Fights rarely start with punches. They start with hurtful words.

"After waiting tables all day, sometimes I wonder where I'm going to find the strength to lead a three-hour class," says Emily, holding a strike pad for a student. "But the energy I pick up from the other women keeps me going."

THANG NGO

INFORMATION TECHNOLOGY CONSULTANT, AGE 30 **CHICAGO, ILLINOIS**

Teaches computer skills to Asian immigrants

PHOTOGRAPHS BY WILLIAM MERCER MCLEOD

The war was going on most of the time during my childhood. We had a house, in Bienhoa, Vietnam, but had to move around a lot in the 1970s as the Communists got closer. One of my brothers, a radio engineer, had to go to reeducation school—really, it was a prison camp. That was a tough time. Learning to follow a new political regime was hard.

But the Vietnamese culture stayed the same, and doing things for others, unrelated to income and business, was part of the culture. My family is still there. My father worked for the Voice of America radio program, and volunteered his time with the church. We never spoke about volunteer philosophy or volunteer spirit; it was just understood, more like neighbors helping out neighbors. I remember there was a fire in three houses, including mine, and all my family and neighbors helped to rebuild our house. We didn't have much money. All we could provide for them was food. My sisters prepared big meals. We had that house built in a month.

That's how I grew up. The community would come together to help people out when they were in need. Everyone knows their neighbor's specialty, how each person can help. We knew who were the masons, and carpenters, and so on. And we didn't have to ask. They came and offered help as soon as they found out. You were looked down upon if you had skills and didn't offer them to help.

I started volunteering here in 1991, in Pittsburgh, when I worked for Westinghouse, a big engineering company. They had a Junior Achievement program set up. I was teaching high school kids about business management, and I learned a lot, too. In college, I was a peer counselor. I think whenever I have a chance to volunteer

"Where I grew up in Vietnam, we all knew it was our responsibility to step forward with certain skills and help out when someone was in need," says Thang. Here he teaches Microsoft Word in his basic-skills computer class at the Chinese Mutual Aid Association in Chicago.

In Thang's class, Khan Phan practices typing a prescription for a Chinese herbal medicine. "What I'm doing here helps me in experience, and it helps the students in their skills," says Thang. "There are no limits to what people, especially children, can do with support from others. I'm living proof of that."

versus do something else, I'll go for the volunteering every time.

This computer class I teach through United Way came about by accident. I happened to stop by the Chinese Mutual Aid Association of Chicago to take a class in Chinese. The teacher said if I teach an English class, I could take the Chinese class for free. I saw a bunch of computers sitting around and asked about them. They were donated from a bank and no one knew if any worked. They weren't hardware people. I just set them up, installed all the software, and connected the network and printers for them. They said I could teach computers and take Chinese for free, but now I don't have time to take the Chinese class. They tell me they're glad I came around.

I have eight students, one in his sixties. It's all new to them. I'm teaching them how to use Microsoft Word. They're all at the intermediate English level, so it's not easy. I speak Vietnamese. No Chinese. It's amazing how much they want to learn and how much they catch on.

I went through the same thing when I was sixteen and came to the United States. I spoke very little English. I learned a little English in a refugee camp in Malaysia; I was there a year and a half. But I went straight into the tenth grade, taking biology and all.

Sometimes the students have blank stares. I know they have questions so I ask what their needs are. Maybe someone will keep advancing and get a computer job somewhere. I didn't speak English, and now I'm working for a good company so I'm not going to rule out any possibility.

It's rewarding to use your knowledge to help others' skills develop. I have a dream to go back to Vietnam and do something in my old community there. They're not as high-tech over there. The education system is pretty good, but there's no hardware available. I think volunteering is not only for me to help the center here; it's also a way for me to learn how to help in general. In Vietnam, they'll have all the same questions my students have now. It's exciting, because I know I could get something like this set up, easy. Equipment in Vietnam is cheap.

My wife is from the Czech Republic and does volunteer work for hospices. She doesn't care if she gets paid for work she loves. I admire that, and it helps us in our marriage. I see her personality through the things she does, how she helps people unconditionally.

I got to this country through volunteer work. My foster family here volunteered their home and time for me. Whatever I do now, I can't forget where I came from.

If you're not sure if volunteering helps people, take a look at your own life, from childhood to where you are now. You'll probably come up with a scenario where someone helped you—someone gave to you expecting nothing in return. It's helped everybody.

AMBER COFFMAN

HIGH SCHOOL STUDENT, AGE 15 **GLEN BURNIE, MARYLAND**

Founder of Happy Helpers for the Homeless

PHOTOGRAPHS BY ELI REED

When my mother suggested we volunteer at Sarah's House, a homeless shelter in Ft. Mead, I was hesitant. I was only eight years old and had a negative mental picture of the homeless. I was even a little scared when I thought about what I'd seen on TV. I thought all homeless people were dirty or sick or drug addicts or insane. But I agreed to go, because I think deep inside, I really did want to help.

When we arrived at the shelter, the negative image I had about homeless people was blown away. I saw kids my age or younger, who looked exactly like me. They dressed and acted like kids I knew in school. We talked, played, and just hung out for the hour or so that I was there. Mom and I were silent on our way home, and there was a warm, good feeling between us. I think we both knew then that volunteering was the right thing to do. I knew that I would keep doing it for the rest of my life.

The trip to Ft. Mead became a weekly event for us. It became our mother and daughter "bonding time." Two years later I started Happy Helpers for the Homeless. Everything that goes into making Happy Helpers work enriches my life and the lives of the other volunteers, not just the homeless people we encounter.

Knowing that the meal you helped prepare and deliver may be the only food another human being receives that day brings an incredible sense of purpose to what you are doing and to your life. People depend on the food we deliver. For me, this means everything we deliver, every meal, should be delivered with love and care. And it is.

Finding donations from markets and bakeries, getting kids and teenagers involved, making the lunches, delivering the food, organizing specials days for the homeless, getting businesses to volunteer services

"People depend on the food we deliver," says Amber, here organizing kids from age six to eighteen in her mother's apartment. On this Saturday afternoon, Amber's group will make more than six hundred sandwiches for homeless families.

like free haircuts—words can't explain how important all of these things have become in my life. It's important because I know it makes a difference, even if it's just a small difference.

Making positive changes a little bit at a time is okay with me. I'm hooked on volunteering. It's part of my everyday life, like going to school or hanging out at the mall with my friends. It's become my way of life. Mother Teresa is the model of giving that I follow. She's my inspiration. She dedicated her entire life to helping those in need.

But it isn't like all of this is so serious for me, either. I have plenty of time to do other normal, teenager-type stuff, too. I played soccer for the first time this year and was the striker, the one who's supposed to score the goals. I never scored

Amber delivers her lunches every Saturday here, at the Harundale Presbyterian Church in Glen Burnie, and at Baltimore's City Hall every Sunday.

once, but I still had fun doing it. I'm in a club at school called the Multicultural Alliance, a big group of kids that gets together to discuss different cultures, racism, and sexism. I don't have a boyfriend right now, but I date occasionally, you know, like going to the movies and stuff.

I don't mind working hard organizing Happy Helpers because I have fun doing it. The people I meet are wonderful. They know me now, so everywhere I go in downtown Baltimore, people say, "Hello, Amber," or "Thank you, Amber."

Last summer this man approached me, a guy in his mid-thirties, I think, who had been on the street for some time. He was really excited, like a kid, jumping up and down when he saw me. He said, "I have a job! I have a job and that's not

"Volunteering is part of my everyday life, like going to school or hanging out with my friends," says Amber. Her group has gathered for 252 consecutive weekends to make meals.

all—I have a place to live." He calmed down, took on a serious tone and said, "This is the last time you'll ever see me. But I have to tell you, it wouldn't have happened without you. I never would have made it without what you do."

That one man's life was changed because of a few volunteers who get together on weekends and just give from the heart. That's what gets me up early when I don't feel like making lunches. I do it because of the wonderful feelings involved with giving. Once you truly give of yourself, you're hooked for life.

The only way to understand what I mean is to go out and do it. I don't think there's any good way to explain the feeling you get when you volunteer for something you believe in. You have to experience that to know what it feels like.

HERNANDO GRUESO

ELECTRICIAN, AGE 53 **STRATFORD, NEW JERSEY**

Renovates homes for low-income families

PHOTOGRAPHS BY ED KASHI

I was raised in a very small town in Colombia, South America. There were no more than twenty-five houses in the whole village. I lost my mother while there, when I was very young and had six brothers and four sisters at the time. But everyone was there to help us out, relatives and close friends. The people there were very close. Somehow you are related to the neighbors like one big family, you know?

Here are some words of wisdom I remember from my mother: "I will plant the seeds, even though I will not collect the fruit from the trees." She was trying to say she would do good and not expect good to come back to her. Her children and family would benefit and it seemed to work. My mother always gave. If people were hungry, if they came around and asked for bread, she would give some to them. Her hope was that if her kids were ever in need and she wasn't there to take care of them, that somebody would help.

I would say the volunteer spirit was alive with us. It was a real community. Everybody pitched in. If someone needed a water well to be dug up, people all got together to do it on one day, all day.

That's how the church was built. Our priest organized this. He refused to lead Mass in our run-down church because it was in such bad shape. I hate to say he worked like a mule, because he's a priest, but he did. He would take off his shirt and collar and sweat, dig trenches, mix cement, and cut wood. He was physically a strong man, and you had no choice but to join him. People stopped and stared when he took off his robe for the first time to work. He would say, "I am a man just like all of you!" You had to respect him.

This guy would refuse to let rich people have hired hands build the church for them. Everyone carried the bricks that built the church. He made everyone carry at least one brick. Children carried just one. Older people, one or two. Young men would carry many.

The priest went on to build beautiful churches all over. He died a poor man. Every cent he collected went right back into the towns. To me that man was a saint. And now for six years or better I've been volunteering for the St. Joseph's Carpenter Society, which was founded by a priest, Monsignor Robert McDermott.

I always volunteered. It doesn't have to be through a church or group. We had a man and his two little girls from a refugee Mexican family

"I like that I'm building something for someone else," says Hernando. "Volunteering helps to build a community. Donate blood. Stop on the side of the road if someone has a flat tire. Do any little thing that will help others."

"What we're doing is making progress a little at a time," says Hernando, who often volunteers with his son, David. "A little progress in this city is better than doing nothing and letting it go completely."

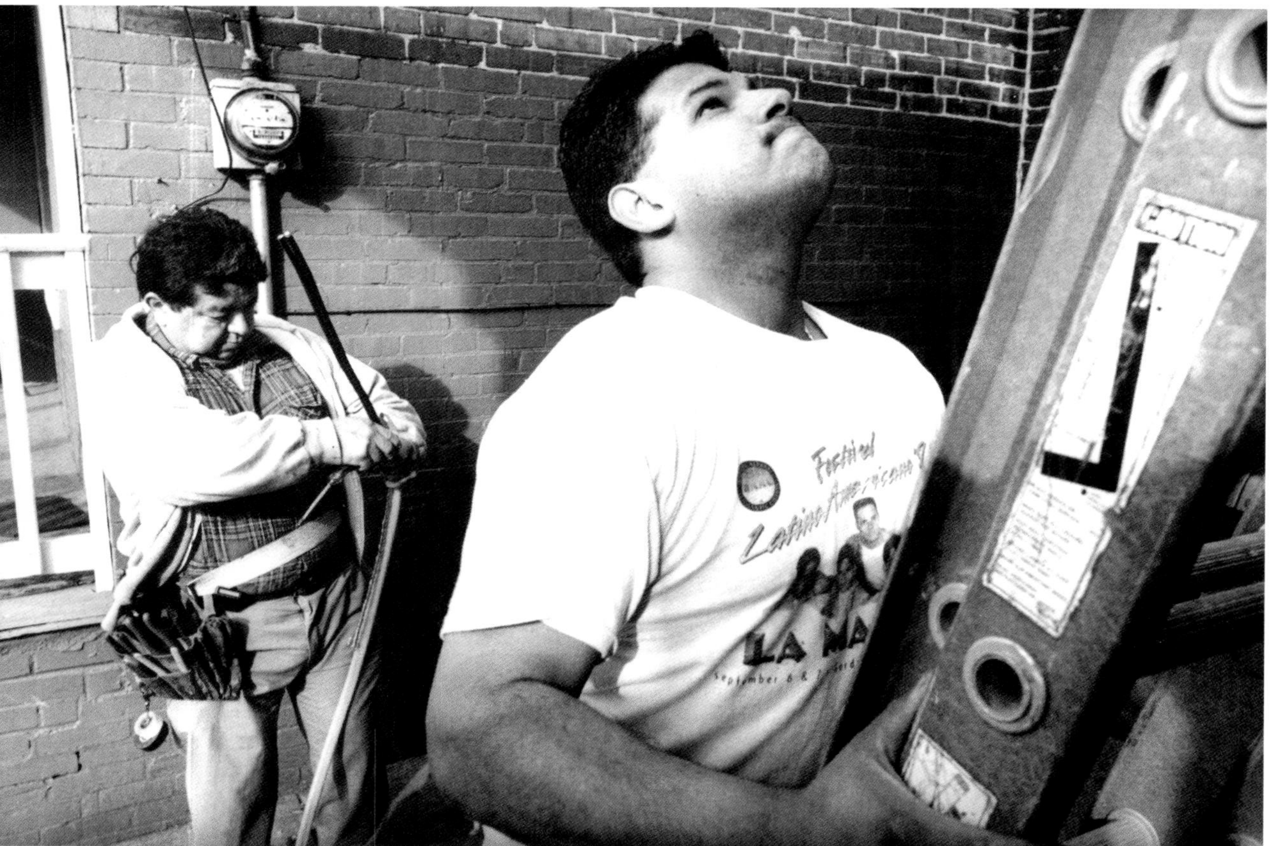

stay at our house. They had no place to stay. He went off to work in New York State and we kept the girls. I'm a guy who will help anybody. It's in my nature.

I hate discrimination and I hate abuse. If someone is having a hard time just because their first language is Spanish, I want to help out. Some people are really helpless in taking care of their apartments. Many don't speak English and can't communicate with landlords and repair people. I feel good when I can help out. It brings back memories of my mother. Her words come to my mind all the time. All the time.

I like volunteering with my son. It is definitely a bonding time for us. And it gives me pleasure to see an old run-down house be rebuilt and a new family living in it.

I like that I'm doing good. I'm following my mother's words. Someday I might need help or some member of my family may need help.

I've learned that giving makes me happy. Jimmy Carter is an inspiration. I would be delighted to work for his organization. I compare him to that priest from my old town in Colombia. He came from a rich family and was president, but he works on houses for the people in his old age. I really admire someone like that.

I'm so happy to see a little progress in this city. So I say volunteer because it makes a difference. Donate blood. Any little thing that will help others. If you want to do it, you make the time.

Hernando installs new electrical wiring for a once abandoned, recently renovated apartment building. Since 1985 the St. Joseph's Carpenter Society has rehabilitated over one hundred homes in East Camden, New Jersey.

BEVERLY BUSHYHEAD-VIVIER

CASE MANAGER, AGE 34 **ST. PAUL, MINNESOTA**

Gives family-to-family mentoring

PHOTOGRAPHS BY ELAINE LITTLE

As parents we want to model certain values to our children: compassion, generosity, patience, time management, problem-solving skills. Everything you want to give to your children, you can show them by volunteering.

Volunteering as a family creates a connection between you and your city, and with people of different races and backgrounds. It creates time as a family when you do something that matters. This is quality family time—and you're not just renting videos.

I've been involved in Family to Family Ties for three years. First, as a participant, when I was homeless and had a four-year-old son, Kyle, and newborn twin girls, Loren and Hana. We got help finding funding for a townhouse, furniture, clothes, Christmas presents, transportation—everything I needed to get back on track. Now I've got a good job, I'm mentoring for Family to Family, and this spring I'm getting my degree in psychology.

I used to think volunteers were people who told you how to live. I used to fear getting help because I feared judgment and was embarrassed about my situation. Now I've learned that volunteers learn as much from the people they help, and that homelessness can happen to anyone. I'm no better than anyone and they're no better than me.

The hardest part of helping a family who's struggling is to help them feel comfortable enough to

"It helps to have someone there for you who has been in the same boat as you," says Kris Swenson (left), here with Beverly. "We have the same ideas on raising children." Kris and her four kids were isolated and on welfare before meeting Beverly through the Family to Family Ties program. "Now," says her mentor, Beverly, "she's a different person."

get out and experience things. The woman I mentor, Kris, has four children. She was on welfare, didn't have money, and didn't leave the house. When you're poor, you live in a neighborhood where there's no YMCA down the street. It's more than not having money—it's not having opportunities that becomes a poverty of spirit. I think there was a shame this family had, and in the beginning we were proving we just wanted to be there for them because they are human beings.

The first thing we provided was transportation and encouragement. It wasn't real to her at first. After taking her child to the doctor and bringing my family over for her children's birthdays, she saw it wasn't just talk, that we were for real and we really cared. At first, she denied needing help. Now she's a different person. She knows how to ask for help and calls me.

Our kids took to each other from the beginning. My son, Kyle, has a long braid and one pierced ear, and Kris's kids had questions about that. When they see stuff in the media about Native Americans, they ask if that bothers me or if it is true. From spending time with us, I think they've learned that Native Americans aren't like what they've seen in the movies, that there are contemporary issues we face and that we have a culture and a strength that helps us survive in this world. We can serve as role models.

Since they learned to trust us, it's like everyone sort of belongs to each other now. We generally get together on the weekends and share a meal. A lot of times Kris will want to talk, so we'll meet somewhere while the kids play together.

Work is a frightening concept to her right now because she hasn't worked in years. Welfare requires her to work, and I'm helping her for the next stage of her life. I'm getting her some business clothes, teaching her how to fill out applications, writing cover letters and resumes. It's a whole new chapter in her life.

One day I visited Kris for a cookout, and I had a problem on my mind. We talked, and she had an insight that really helped me deal with it. This was a few months into the relationship, and I truly didn't expect that. Our roles reversed, and I realized that the role of mentor would blur and go back and forth. I think it was empowering for Kris and changed the whole tone of our relationship. After that when I'd call and say, "Let me know if you need anything," she'd say, "You too."

"People talk about spending quality family time," says Beverly (right). "This is it." Beverly's son, Kyle (standing), and daughter Loren (sitting, far right) spend the day with the Swenson family at the Como Park Conservatory.

One of the biggest lessons I've learned is that everyone has something to give. Even when you think you're the one in the giving role, you get as much as you give. Sometimes it's hard to see who's the mentor. Maybe you can't change the world, but you really can change a piece of someone's world just through caring. It's incredible what single mothers can do when they believe in themselves and someone believes in them.

I was in Kris's situation for a long time. So many people helped me get to where I am now. Teachers helped. Friends helped. People stepped forward who became friends. My mentors from this program gave my life back to me. I didn't have dreams; I was just trying to survive.

Volunteering is what I do with my life. It's how my family lives. People who don't volunteer can't imagine how good it feels or they don't think it makes a difference.

I would tell those people my story. Where I was then and where I am now, it's a dream. It has everything to do with people who volunteered. Complete strangers. People who didn't know me at all gave me my life and my dreams again.

"At first I only saw Sharif when my mom would go over to their house," says Kyle, here wrestling with Sharif in Beverly's house. "Then we had a snowball fight, and we've gotten along well ever since. We both like baseball and slow jazz."

Getting Involved in Service and Its Satisfactions

BRIAN O'CONNELL

I'm surprised when I hear people say that they want to get involved but the opportunities just don't seem to come along. My surprise doubles when I hear organization leaders express frustration that they can't find people to volunteer. Both the individuals and the causes are going without the value of the participation.

This section of the book is intended for people not now involved in volunteer service and its satisfactions. It will also be useful for those not participating as much or in ways that they want.

We need to be more helpful in guiding people into voluntary activity. I hope the volunteers portrayed in this book help provide motivation and examples of ways to help. These examples should also assure people that there are roles and rewards for everyone.

As Julie Cotton says: *Everyone has talents. You have to find what yours are and then volunteer with that.*

Amber Coffman adds: *The only way to understand what I mean is to go out and do it. I don't think there's any good way to explain the feeling you get when you volunteer for something you believe in. You have to experience that to know what it feels like.*

Katherine Pener summarizes her experience: *You don't have to have gone through what the people you help have gone through. You just need to give your time, that's all. Don't worry about whether you can do it or not. Get out and help out. You help a human being, and that person is going to be grateful. You'll be proud of yourself, and your family will be so proud of what you do.*

Jim Humphrey ended his interview: *Everyone should give volunteering a try. You'll be surprised by what you have to offer. It only takes one or two hours a week to make a difference. Any nonprofit can use the help. Do something.*

Sometimes those who are not volunteering worry that they won't be dedicated enough or able to give all the time that's expected. Certainly some of the wonderful examples in this book could reinforce a sense that, by comparison, our own efforts might be inadequate.

Nothing could be further from the truth. Indeed, it is the composite of all the volunteering that leads to the compassion, spirit, and power that are characteristic of voluntary action in America. The important thing is that a great many people are involved in all kinds of causes, and they have many opportunities to influence their own lives and be of service to others. Today, anyone who cares and is prepared to do something about it can make a difference.

A man we can identify no further than by his good name, Henry Van Dyke, said, "Use what talents you possess. The woods would be very silent if no birds sung except those that sang best."

But often the question we hear is, "How do I get involved?" First of all, you can't assume that out of the blue someone is going to ask you to take on some fascinating project and away you'll go. The reality is that the largest single reason people do not volunteer is that no one has asked them. If you're not already involved but would be willing to do some volunteer work, you are probably going to have to do some scouting. For many, that starts with one's own religious organization or with religiously affiliated services in the community such as Catholic Charities, the local Jewish Federation, or The Salvation Army. Don't hesitate to call or stop by to explore what volunteer assignments they might know about. With each contact you'll learn more about volunteering and about other groups in the community that utilize volunteers. Here are some specific places to start.

1. An increasing number of communities have Voluntary Action Centers (VAC), which help to bring together organizations that need volunteers and people who are willing to give time. VAC's already recruit and place more than a half million new volunteers annually and provide training for them. Find out if your community has a VAC.

The Points of Light Foundation, which serves as the coordinating body for the country's large network of VAC's, has a toll free telephone number to help connect you with the Center nearest you. Give it a try. It's 1-800-VOLUNTEER.

If it turns out that there isn't a VAC near you, you might even think about what you could do to get one going to help make connections

between people like you and the many organizations that need volunteers.
2. Contact your local United Way. They're in almost every part of the country. They can tell you if there is a VAC, which of their member organizations regularly use volunteers and what kinds of assignments there are. They will also know many other organizations in the community that may not be affiliated formally with United Way but with which they work.
3. Service clubs, fraternal groups and the like not only become involved in volunteer assignments themselves but know of groups that are regularly turning to them for volunteers.
4. Don't hesitate to explore your interest with your elected representatives and other public office holders. They know the community well and are often the best source of information about who needs help for what types of causes, or you may want to consider becoming involved in a political campaign. Often your community's elected and appointed leaders can suggest projects to help with bond issues, volunteer services within government and other activities that even sophisticated volunteer leaders don't know exist.
5. It's also a good idea to talk to school principals and other school personnel, who are likely to know of causes in their areas. Local colleges are often looking for volunteers, either within the institution itself or through the outreach activities of professors who are engaged in special studies in the community.
6. Librarians are often overlooked but are an obvious source of guidance. They know of needs within the library system itself but they also know a great deal about what's going on throughout the areas they serve.
7. It's a good idea to talk also with editors and radio and TV station managers (and certainly public service directors where that posi-

tion exists). They, like several of the other groups mentioned above, are at the crossroads of a great deal of community information and are likely to surprise you with their ready knowledge of organizations that need help.

Beyond these general contacts, go directly to organizations and facilities where you think you might like to be involved. That can include the hospital, Red Cross, American Heart Association, historical society, Humane Society, library, community college, Scouts, public radio and TV stations, community foundation, community health center, Easter Seal Society, and scores of other groups. You may even find them in the Yellow Pages under "nonprofit," "voluntary," or "social service organizations."

To test this advice I looked in the phone book of the new and relatively small community to which we recently moved and was delighted to find almost a full page devoted just to "Social and Human Services," including fifteen categories of associations such as youth and elderly, and more than forty specific organizations including addresses and phone numbers.

Don't get discouraged if the first few contacts don't provide specific assignments, or even if the first assignments aren't exactly what you hoped for. Keep plugging at it, and you'll gradually—maybe even suddenly—find yourself involved in satisfying service.

Don't be unwilling to start with fairly routine tasks. Most voluntary organizations are so hungry for interested, able people, that your show of interest and effective handling of initial tasks will quickly lead to interesting responsibilities. Many people hold out for leadership posts right from the start and generally end up waiting forever. It's the person who is willing to dive in who will rise to those leadership ranks.

Many people who are older and have more leisure time want to have some fascinating, challenging, and perhaps prestigious assignments. But they may be quick to turn down the kind of assignments that usually represent an entry-level participation. I'm with volunteer leaders a lot and know that their friends and others envy them, but won't get started themselves. My constant advice is for people to dive in somewhere, and I hold out the likelihood that they'll find the contacts and the work sufficiently stimulating to make it all worthwhile.

Because I've learned repeatedly that even motivated people need specific examples of what causes they might want to connect with, I'm going to provide below more information than most readers will really want to bother with but which might just serve up the right possibilities for others.

Please forgive the detail, but there is a lot to cover, and even this will only be a sampling of what INDEPENDENT SECTOR calls its classification of types of nonprofit organizations.

ARTS AND CULTURAL ORGANIZATIONS—includes museums (natural history, science, art), film and video, singing societies, and literary presses.

EDUCATIONAL INSTITUTIONS—includes vocational, libraries, dropout prevention, adult education, and school athletics.

ENVIRONMENT—includes pollution control (air, water, noise), recycling, land conservation, historic preservation, and outdoor survival.

ANIMALS—includes animal welfare, aquariums, fisheries, zoos, and endangered species.

HEALTH, GENERAL AND REHABILITATIVE—includes hospitals, sexuality education, rehabilitation services, blood supply, and ambulances.

MENTAL HEALTH AND CRISIS PREVENTION—includes multipurpose centers, group homes, hotlines, and treatment of gambling addiction.

DISEASE/DISABILITIES—includes learning disabilities, arthritis, sickle cell anemia, Alzheimer's, and cancer.

CONSUMER PROTECTION—includes legal services, court administration, public interest litigation, and consumer protection and safety.

CRIME AND DELINQUENCY—includes delinquency prevention, missing persons services, probation/parole programs, dispute resolution, and family violence.

EMPLOYMENT/JOBS—includes vocational education, occupational health and safety, employment training, and sheltered workshops.

FOOD, NUTRITION, AND AGRICULTURE—includes botanical gardens, farmers cooperatives, farmland preservation, food banks, meals on wheels, home economics, and hunger.

HOUSING/SHELTER—includes public housing, housing search assistance, temporary shelters, homeowners associations, and tenants organizations.

PUBLIC SAFETY, DISASTER PREPAREDNESS, AND RELIEF—includes relief services, civil defense, flood control, fire prevention, and safety education.

RECREATION/LEISURE/SPORTS—includes youth centers, scouting organizations, senior centers, parks and playgrounds, hobby clubs, and amateur sports competitions.

YOUTH DEVELOPMENT—includes mentoring programs, Big Brothers/Big Sisters, foster grandparent programs, and scouting organizations.

HUMAN SERVICES—includes The Red Cross, YMCAs and YWCAs, adoption services, foster care, family services, transportation, and developmentally disabled centers.

INTERNATIONAL AND FOREIGN AFFAIRS—includes human rights, international understanding, cultural exchange, relief services, and peace.

CIVIL RIGHTS AND SOCIAL ACTION—includes immigrant rights, disabled persons, seniors rights, intergroup race relations, voter education, and civil liberties.

COMMUNITY IMPROVEMENT—includes civic centers, economic development, visitor/convention bureaus, better business bureaus, and service clubs.

PHILANTHROPY, VOLUNTARISM, AND GRANTMAKING FOUNDATIONS—includes community foundations, voluntarism promotion, corporate-related foundations, and public services.

SCIENCE, TECHNOLOGY, AND SOCIAL SERVICE RESEARCH—includes observatories, interdisciplinary research centers, and scientific research.

PUBLIC/SOCIETY BENEFIT—includes veterans organizations, transportation systems, cooperatives, credit unions, and Native American tribes and governments.

RELIGION AND SPIRITUALITY—includes churches, mosques, synagogues, and religiously affiliated services.

MUTUAL/MEMBERSHIP BENEFIT ORGANIZATIONS—includes insurance, pension trusts, fraternal societies, cemeteries, and burial services.

Check your own favorite dozen or so and then ask around about organizations in your community that might be among those types.

If there are some people who can't find anything in this list to turn them on, then even this inveterate optimist has to accept that maybe they should stay in their rocking chairs.

For those who are intrigued with various possibilities, go on the hunt. Even if you don't find that specific organization dealing with care of small animals, you might find one that protects endangered species, or if you don't locate one that covers historic preservation, you may become fascinated with the programs of your local historical society. There are lots of matches out there for you.

For a lighter sampling of the almost endless possibilities, here is a delightful list put together by Waldemar Nielsen, one of the country's best observers of voluntary action.

"If your interest is people, you can help the elderly by a contribution to the Grey Panthers; or teenagers through the Jean Teen Scene of Chicago; or young children through your local nursery school; or everyone by giving to the Rock of All Ages in Philadelphia.

"If your interest is animals, there is the ASPCA and Adopt-a-Pet; if fishes, the Izaak Walton League; if birds, the American Homing Pigeon Institute or the Easter Bird Banding Association.

"If you are interested in tradition and social continuity, there is the Society for the Preservation of Historic Landmarks and the Portland Friends of Cast Iron Architecture; if social change is your passion, there is Common Cause; and, if that seems too sober for you, there is the Union of Radical Political Economists or perhaps the Theatre for Revolutionary Satire.

"If your pleasure is music, there is a supermarket of choices—from Vocal Jazz to the Philharmonic Society to the American Guild of English Hand Bellringers.

"If you don't know quite what you want there is Get Your Head Together, Inc., of Glen Ridge, New Jersey. If your interests are contradictory, there is the Great Silence Broadcasting Foundation of California. If they are ambiguous, there is the Tombstone Health Service of Arizona."

There are obviously many possibilities to explore, and even a modest search is likely to provide rewarding connections for you and the causes you decide to serve.

PHOTOGRAPHERS & PHOTO CREDITS

JOE BUISSINK has published his photographs in the *Los Angeles Times, LA Weekly, Gourmet, People, In Style,* and *American Photo.* He works in a wide array of photographic styles, from advertising and portraiture to album covers and film. Joe also documents celebrity weddings and recently shot the stills for the 1998 Academy Award–nominated documentary film *Colors Straight Up.* Photograph on front cover, center, and on pages 40–45 and 108–13 © Joe Buissink.

CHIEN-CHI CHANG joined Magnum Photos in 1995. He was awarded a degree in English language and literature at Soochow University, Taiwan, in 1984, and continued his studies at Indiana University in 1990. His work has been published in *National Geographic, Fortune,* and *Time,* and presented in collective exhibitions at the International Center of Photography and the South Street Seaport Museum in New York. Photographs on pages 134–39 © Chien-Chi Chang/Magnum Photos.

JOHN EISELE is a freelance photographer in Fort Collins, Colorado, specializing in photography of people on location for editorial and corporate clients. Before moving to Colorado in 1997, he spent nine years as a staff photographer for *National Journal* magazine in Washington, D.C., photographing politicians, attorneys, and lobbyists. Photographs on pages 60–65, 82–85, and 100–103 © John Eisele.

LEONARD FREED was first associated with Magnum Photos in 1956 and became a full member in 1972. Known for his work covering black America, events in Israel, and the Yom-Kippur War, he continues to photograph in Europe, Africa, Asia, and the United States. His books include *Black in White America; Off Limits; Made in Germany; Police Work; New York Police; Leonard Freed: Photographies 1954-1990;* and *Amsterdam.* Photographs on pages 96–99 © Leonard Freed/Magnum Photos.

PAUL FUSCO joined Magnum Photos in 1973 after receiving a degree in photojournalism at the University of Ohio in 1957. Until 1971 he worked as a staff photographer for *Look* magazine, becoming known for his studies of homeless people and of alternative lifestyles. His books include *Sense Relaxation: Below the Mind; La Causa: The California Grape Strike; What to Do Until the Messiah Comes;* and *The Photo Essay: Paul Fusco & Will McBride.* Photograph on back cover and on pages 18–23, 30–35, 46–49, and 90–95 © Paul Fusco/Magnum Photos.

DIRCK HALSTEAD is *Time* magazine's Senior White House Photographer in Washington, D.C. Halstead's awards include the Robert Capa Gold Medal of the Overseas Press Club, First Prize in Documentary for the Pictures of the Year, and nine first-place awards from the White House Press Photographers Association. In 1997, he created an online magazine, *The Digital Journalist.* Photographs on pages 104–107 © Dirck Halstead.

ED KASHI has published his photographs in *National Geographic, The New York Times Sunday Magazine, Time, Fortune, Geo, Smithsonian, London Independent Magazine, Natural History, The Atlantic Monthly, Audubon, Grata,* and *Aperture.* He has covered subjects from the heroin problem in Poland to the return of Soviet vets from the Afghan war, and since 1991 has focused on issues in the Middle East for *National Geographic.* His books are *The Protestants: No Surrender* and *When the Borders Bleed: The Struggle of the Kurds.* Photograph on front cover, right, and on pages 54–59, 118–23, 128–33, and 148–53 © Ed Kashi.

ELAINE LITTLE has documented the plight and promise of children, families, and communities in more than twenty countries. Her photographs have been exhibited at the United Nations and World Economic Forum and used by UNICEF and the Children's Defense Fund. Elaine's award-winning work on family violence was featured in a Bill Moyers special on youth and violence. She recently completed her first book, *Children of the Philippines.* Photograph on front cover, left, and on pages 66–71 and 154–59 © Elaine Little.

ALEX MAJOLI joined Magnum Photos in 1996. He began working full time on social documentary projects in 1988 for the Unitalpress and Double agencies in Milan, Italy, as well as Gamma in Paris. His most recent project looks at the treatment of patients in a psychiatric hospital in Sarajevo in the wake of war. Photographs on pages 24–29 © Alex Majoli/Magnum Photos.

WILLIAM MERCER MCLEOD studied literature and film at U.C. Berkeley and the University of Paris III, and now specializes in portraiture and reportage for books and magazines such as *Time, Life,* and *Wired.* Much of his work revolves around children, including his current project on foster care and adoption. Photographs on pages 72–77 and 140–43 © William Mercer McLeod.

ELI REED joined Magnum Photos in 1983 after being a runner-up for the Pulitzer Prize in 1981. He has covered events in Central America and Beirut, as well as gangs in Detroit. His awards include a Neiman Scholarship from Harvard University, the Nikon World Understanding Award, the Overseas Press Club Award, the World Press Award, and the W. Eugene Smith Grant. His books are *Beirut: City of Regrets* and *Black in America.* Photographs on pages 36–39 and 144–47 © Eli Reed/Magnum Photos.

ALEX WEBB joined Magnum Photos in 1974 after studying history and literature at Harvard University. He was awarded the Leopold Godowsky Jr. Prize for color photography in 1988. His books include *Hot Light, Half-Made Worlds: Photographs from the Tropics; Under a Grudging Sun: Photographs from Haiti Libéré 1986–1989; From the Sunshine State: Photographs from Florida; Amazon: From the Floodplains to the Clouds;* and *Dislocations.* Photographs on pages 78–81 and 114–17 © Alex Webb/Magnum Photos.

MANY THANKS to Brian O'Connell, Lynn D. W. Luckow, and Caroline Herter for inviting me to join this project. To David Strettell at Magnum and all the photographers: thank you for seeing the big heart of this book, for taking red-eye flights to points unknown, and for bringing us back great images. To Carole Goodman and Anne Galperin: you're the best. Thanks also to Jula Falvey, Douglass Fischer, Vanessa Brown, David Salniker, Dahnesh Medora, Justin Probert, Kevin Miller, and Bob Kosturak. To Thomas Moore, thank you for saying yes. And thank you to all the volunteers who let us in on their moments of giving.

REBECCA TAYLOR